D1105936

CLIF SANDERSON

Knowing Nothing, Living Happy

Illustrations by
STEFAN STUTZ

A Deep Field Relaxation Book

www.intention-in-action.com
clifsanderson@yahoo.co.uk
www.stefanstutz.de

Deep Field Relaxation is not a therapy
but a way of life.
Clif Sanderson is not medically trained and he
insists people with health concerns consult the
qualified therapist of their choice.

Note for Librarians: A cataloguing record for this book is available from Library and Archives
Canada at www.collectionscanada.ca/amicus/index-e.html
ISBN 1-4251-0560-2

Printed in Victoria, BC, Canada. Printed on paper with minimum 30% recycled fibre.
Trafford's print shop runs on "green energy" from solar, wind and other environmentally-friendly power sources.

TRAFFORD
PUBLISHING™
Offices in Canada, USA, Ireland and UK

Book sales for North America and international:
Trafford Publishing, 6E–2333 Government St.,
Victoria, BC V8T 4P4 CANADA
phone 250 383 6864 (toll-free 1 888 232 4444)
fax 250 383 6804; email to orders@trafford.com
Book sales in Europe:
Trafford Publishing (UK) Limited, 9 Park End Street, 2nd Floor
Oxford, UK OX1 1HH UNITED KINGDOM
phone +44 (0)1865 722 113 (local rate 0845 230 9601)
facsimile +44 (0)1865 722 868; info.uk@trafford.com
Order online at:
trafford.com/06-2318

10 9 8 7 6 5 4 3 2 1

One of the unmistakable signs
of spiritual awareness is the
cheerful capacity to say, 'I was
wrong', and it will save us a lot
of trouble in life if we can make
that very daring statement,

'We don't know'.

Eknath Easwaran

~ Selfless service to others is a source of joy ~
Gandhi

Contents

Preface

In many of the islands of the majestic Pacific Ocean, Polynesian-speaking people often greet each other by announcing their *karakia*.

My own welcome begins...

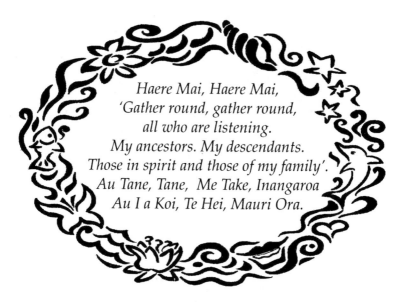

Haere Mai, Haere Mai,
'Gather round, gather round,
all who are listening.
My ancestors. My descendants.
Those in spirit and those of my family'.
Au Tane, Tane, Me Take, Inangaroa
Au I a Koi, Te Hei, Mauri Ora.

It includes respect for the land I am standing on, especially if I am a stranger.

It is a recognition of my ancestors and, if we are speaking to a large group, it gives the background of who I am. Only then can I be heard.

For it is in the speaking and the telling of stories that each of us can find ourselves. Stories of experiences, some stories true and imagined; some teach through metaphors, others just good creative poems of joy and love between families to brighten and amuse.

Maybe they are about the power of not knowing, or the mystery of personal transformation, perhaps an easy way to discover why we are born, why we are here and what to do with this greatest of all gifts.

Above all else they are not to be taken too seriously for our minds can easily decipher the truth from the chaff. A joke well told is worth a year of philosophical study.

1. Slightly out
of True

I love hearing stories, I love telling stories. I have never had a guru; avatars leave me cold; there is nothing for me in the jargon of the academic. Life is for loving, breathing is for jumping, dancing, ignoring the artificial fears of the news peddlers. Textbooks divert our attention from the pleasure of watching the dawn, the emotion of the glory of a scarlet sunset; the incredible, unbelievable colour of a tiny flower. Optimism has no place in my life – it diverts us from the truth of being alive and conscious now, that's enough. Today is another day in paradise. Breathe in breathe out. Ahhh. Stories should all begin.......

Once upon a time....................

Three-year-old Sasha lived with his mother, alcoholic father and about 150 other relatives crowded into a tiny apartment in an industrial slum in Moscow.

He suffered from cerebral palsy and had never

had the power in his muscles to sit up, let alone walk. In all other ways he was an intelligent, happy boy.

When his mother came into the room where I was seeing patients, she glanced around and started to leave, discouraged by the heat, the smell of the open sewer outside the window and the depressing view of the nearby oil refinery.

'All I have left is hope,' she said with a hopeless sigh, 'because I have tried everything I could and nothing has worked'.

But Sasha wasn't having any of it. He lay down with a big bright smile as though the sun had been created just for him.

His little round face and intense blue eyes watched everything I did. He couldn't speak English and I only had a few Russian words so we nodded a lot and made silly faces and slowly drifted into quietness.

Then I heard him quietly talking to himself. At first I could only just hear him but I did know the word he was repeating over and over, 'Khoroshor, Khoroshor', 'so good, so goooood, sooo goooood'.

He and his mother came several times over the next few weeks. Slowly there was a change until the day when we saw that his mum's fears had been replaced by tears of joy as he proudly sat up then stood by the edge of the bed. The delighted look on his face that day was a picture - like a crawling baby who suddenly finds himself walking.

She even had another great story to tell. One

time when they got home from the clinic he told his grandmother, 'Babushka, I am Clif, lie down and I will heal your aches and pains.'

What *is* clear is that together we had given nature a chance to do what She is best at doing. Nature likes everything to work out for the best.

Or as Einstein said, Nature always tends towards harmony.

When we begin to understand that immutable Law we can let miracles happen without bothering our ego or troubling our conditioned mind.

For Sasha then, nobody did anything unusual! Nobody was a special person! The time, the place and the surroundings for Sasha's change came together to create a totally appropriate outcome.

In this book we want to take a close look at ways to bridge that gap between logic, practicality, the educated mind and the freedom of acknowledging the mystical, the strange, the unexplainable and the spiritual side of life.

We will find that anyone can create miracles! It takes courage. But with clear intention and a heap of laughter it is all possible! At first it sounds completely impossible. Good!

Because even when we vigorously deny it, magic still happens.

Whether you are on the train or not, it still leaves on time full of happy passengers. Your ticket to ride is priceless. No amount of money can buy it; no travel agent can sell it to you. The paradox is, it costs nothing.

Our journey begins in the magical world of stories.

Let's get started.

How would it be, we sometimes secretly ask ourselves, if we had kept dreaming those dreamy childhood 'if only' wishes?

What if we played with the idea of creating our own world just as we did when we were kids?

It sounds wonderfully dangerous!

Will you play the game with me?

We can't get into trouble doing that, can we? But if problems and awkward questions start to arise then you can just quote my mother! She would take away our childish fears and worries by saying, 'Everything will work out, don't worry, *it will all be the same in a hundred years time!*'

She was a great quoter and an amazing writer!

Night after night she would put her six children to bed and then bring out her old steel typewriter and, far into the dark of night, we would hear her hammering out her 20 novels, mysteries, love stories, children's books and many, many radio plays.

As a child I was haunted for years by a radio series she wrote called, *'Slightly Out of True'* – about those unexplainable things which happen just out of reach of reason. It was a sort of *'X- Files'* without pictures!

Stories endlessly flowed out of her pen and we learnt never to ask whether they were 'true' or not.

What freedom it gave us! Stories can be whatever we want them to be.

We do not have to adopt some sort of common belief system. Instead of giving up our common sense to fit into some guru's pocket, we only have to realize that there is more to this universe than we were ever taught.

No, if we want to have a fascinating life, we have to forget that old stuff.

Why don't we, together, skip the mundane world and try for some magic? There's no fun if we always have to fit into the 'scientific' straight jacket!

Just because something is not explained doesn't mean it is unexplainable. Miracles are like that.

You know what? Nobody can explain why electricity runs down the wire; if you fall off your bike at high speed you have no doubt that gravity somehow exists; and here's a good one, why on earth does the planet keep rotating on a more or less fixed axis which we can't see, touch, smell or feel?

There's nobody out there oiling the wheels, if you know what I mean.

In truth we know very little. Mostly we live here on the planet like alien tenants.

2. The Pilot's Logbook

This next is the story which began a whole new chapter of my life.

As a young man I had three passions. Photography, art and aeroplanes (OK, other passions came along later).

One of the exercises to get a pilot's licence was to fly from home base to an aerodrome more than 80 kilometres away, land there, wait half an hour, then fly home.

As I took off at eight in the morning, I could see it was one of those magic early spring days. A little frost on the ground, not a cloud in the sky.

I turned to fly south with the majesty of the sparkling snow of New Zealand's Southern Alps under the starboard wing of my happy little Piper PA18. On the left, the exquisite blue of the Pacific framing a patchwork of Irish-green sheep pasture and the ripe, deep blacks of ploughed fields.

Then, things began to change. Twenty minutes into the outward journey, my watch stopped.

This, by itself, didn't present any problems. I flew on and landed normally.

Then it dawned on me that I had not seen any other aircraft in the air. There were no cars in the parking lot. There should have been people in the offices. The hangars were shut as though everyone had gone to the moon.

In the eerie silence I saw no point waiting on the ground for the planned half hour and took off within ten minutes.

Once in the air with the sun at my back everything seemed to return to normal.

But it wasn't. When I landed the Chief Flying Instructor came striding across the tarmac towards me.

'Where have you been?' He demanded, 'you are

so late back we had to alert the search and rescue team. That's a ninety-minute flight and you're an hour beyond that!'

This was my first experience of a time slip. My personal Bermuda Triangle.

It couldn't be argued with.

How curious! How interesting!

In the end, with a little smile, I entered the 'correct' time in my Pilot's Logbook as a simple fact.

Of course from then on I was hesitant to take passengers along whenever I flew!

We have all had these things happen. Usually we either ignore them, then swat them away like summer flies or imagine we are on the edge of insanity! Some people, can you imagine, say such things have never happened for them!

What it forced me to start asking was, if it has ever happened anywhere, at any time, for anyone, it must be a Law for everyone. It cannot just work for a few lucky whackos!

There can be no exceptions to the rules. No one travels first class. We are all bundled up together in economy class.

If you want to see if it will happen for you, or it has already happened and you want to increase the frequency here is my suggestion.

>> THINGS TO DO (Notes with this symbol are gathered together in Chapter 36, 'Reminders')

Get a good notebook. One that will travel comfortably inside your pocket or purse wherever you go. The best I know of are the legendary Moleskines.

They were the favourites of Van Gogh, Matisse, Hemingway and Chatwin. Good company to be in if you are serious about your creative development.

They have a neat little elastic band and an inside pocket to hold all the scribbles and doodles of thoroughly original ideas which will spring into mind as you contemplate life, the universe and everything.

I never leave home without one.

To do it truly, you have to become annoying with it! In the middle of a meal, in the middle of a telephone conversation, in bed even. Because you must get into the habit of taking notes at all hours. Even in the most inconvenient and inappropriate places. Alas, unless you catch the thought immediately, by the morning it will have gone. Evaporated.

This is the raw material to be absorbed, re-evaluated, arranged then written into your notebook.

What we need is to create a little space in the monkey chatter of our lives.

It is not important what comes to mind. No struggles, no earth-shattering revelations, no effort.

Just sit holding the notebook in one hand, a pen in the other.

Wait! Wait! I thought of something...no it's gone.

Sit for a few more minutes.

Nothing?

Don't be concerned.

We have plenty of time.

Still nothing?

Put the notebook back in your pocket. Go and dig the garden, clean the car, cook a good meal. Your request has been registered in the giant logbook in the sky. Within days, even hours, you will remember a good story from your vast experience.

Practise and practise. Keep an open mind. It takes courage to turn your educated mind upside down. It will revolt at every corner!

Hey, wait a minute; I just had a great idea. Why not, instead of a notebook make an effort to find an actual Pilot's Logbook?

Flight 101: Flight Plan, Cockpit Check and debriefing

Before each flight each pilot must file a Flight Plan with the Control Tower. The collective brains up there tell you of potential storms on your path, your best height to fly, they guide you around every imaginable problem. Next, you have to do a pre-flight Cockpit Check. Finally, after landing, everyone does their own debriefing - make a short report of the events happened during the flight.

1. Have your logbook at your side. A favourite pen at the ready?
2. Check that you are relaxed, comfortable. Mental seat belt clicked.
3. Headphones on the ears to hear the music of the spheres, or the commands from the higher self
4. It's the day off for your spirit guides so it is up to you to decide the direction to take.
5. Open your brand new logbook.
6. On the left, just *inside* the outer cover, paste a copy of your photo. One that was taken at a special time of your life when you were the happiest. From then on, whenever you open

your pilot's logbook, you will be greeted by lovely you.

7. Smile to yourself. Handsome, beautiful. Soooo lucky!

8. Leave *two* blank pages – this both reminds you of the unlimited potential spaces and the choices you can make.

9. On the next page (it is a right hand page) write your own name. Oh, no, not just with a blunt pencil or a grunchy pen. Take the whole page and an hour or two. Coloured pens, watercolour paints, favourite dried leaves, strings of bright wool. There is no such thing as a person who is not an artist. No one judges except yourself. And this is for yourself. Cover the whole page with your name.

10. By now the cockpit dials have all lit up waiting for the lift off.

11. Lift the pen and begin writing.

12. Write the date and precise time.

13. What, as a child were you fascinated with? Some strange happening perhaps.

....

14. Write as much as you can, letting your pen talk for you.

....

15. Recall one of those day-dreamings.

....

16. Have you ever felt time skip for

you?

. . . .

17. What resistances are you discovering...?

. . . .

18. Any other thoughts.

. . . .

19. Take as long as you wish then place your logbook in your lap, close your eyes and listen outwardly to all the sounds around. Play the *Mind Music* CD to balance your memories.

Later when you return to the tarmac, take out your logbook again and make a note of physical, emotional, spiritual and imagined changes.

Congratulations! You have successfully flown solo for the first time. Keep the aerobatics for later; everyone begins with a closed circuit of the mind. No cross-country flying yet, just a short touch-and-go take off and landing.

3. The Uncharted Waters

Can it be that you have a fear of flying?

Perhaps your fancy takes you closer to the sea. The swashbuckling bravado of the pirate; the adventures of salt-encrusted explorers of the oceans; the smells of the oaken deck below the faded canvas stretching out for new horizons.

Every child's adventure story begins on the high seas of their imagination. None were galley slaves, none the deck scrubbers. Each were, in their minds the pilot of the ship.

He or she were the Captain of their destiny, a child of the universe, bravely facing the dangerous shoals, the sand banks and life-threatening reefs. It was a faithful duty to daily write the logbook recording the disappointments and the triumphs.

The pilot lived and died by the power of the storms which could tear a ship to pieces in an instant; the utter horror of being lost in an endlessly becalmed sea.

His log became the story of the ship, the lives of the crew; the trials, the difficulties, the deaths and the sudden moments of enlightenment as the sun might catch the pearly-green wave crests.

It was hard, constant work.

If sometimes he didn't know where he was on his journey, he learnt to trust.

In our own story, if we listen for it, there comes a miraculous day when our own ship sails into harbour.

We hear the welcoming trumpets of the curious, envious, sleepy crowds; themselves unable to face the rigours of life outside the safety of ritual, dogmatic society.

Now, there is time to relax at home, open your precious log and in the quiet days, read again of all the years of frustration, delusions, difficulties and triumphs.

Finally, as if by magic, you discover you can decipher the pirate's treasure map. Hidden in those scrawls and lost poems of your life there is a clear plan. One that you knew of all along but had never understood.

There is no longer a medley of confusions. In amazement you see that these were not troubles after all.

Just gentle proddings from the Master Teacher.

With a deep sigh of contentment, you find at

last that you are truly home. The successful
navigator of rough seas and far-flung shores.

Your reward is to discover yourself in the
deep ocean currents and the whims of the swirling
air.

4.The Insurance Man

But, like most of us, I needed some clear experience before I woke up to this reality.

Even though flying never left me, art stepped in and I learnt, and suffered from, the loneliness of the artist. The blank canvas, the empty easel, the first words of a poem.

But nevertheless it made me happy to be running my design studio. Maybe the ego was a little overexcited but I was young, I was married with two marvellous children. And I was my own boss (I thought!).

There were posters to do and silk-screen printing, animated films for television, some portraits to paint and lots and lots of stories to write.

Then, just when you think everything is peachy, along comes something without your agreement or conscious desire. Have you noticed?

Well, for me, along came Reg Duder, a shortish,

round sort of a fellow with a kindly smile. He was keen to sell me some insurance. How would I know that he would tell me how to get parking spaces and much more?

'Reg', I said, 'I do not have time for you now as I must make the bank before it closes and it is incredibly difficult to get a parking space this late in the day'.

'Nothing to worry about then, I'll run you there,' hoping for the time to convince me to buy.

It was, after all, just a short drive to the bank in Cathedral Square, Christchurch.

Once in the car, half listening, I heard him say, 'If you are in business you are not in business unless you know about Tulip, all successful salesmen know about Tulip'.

'Yeah. Sure. Thanks Reg.' We are busy looking for a parking space and he's talking religious instruction.

'Tulip looks after business people', he insisted, 'she'll help you find parking spaces, makes those contracts come in, staff happy...things like that'.

In the busiest street in town, still talking, he pulled into a space right outside the bank. Impressive!

But I still remained sceptical. Nevertheless several days later I was desperate for a parking place. I tried it out.

Can you believe that that day and for the rest of the year Tulip arranged a parking space for me?! Not only for the bank but in many other places as well.

vYou can try it yourself.
I guarantee you will be amazed.

The practice is to let go of old beliefs and allow new ways of connecting with the powerful forces of the universe, which naturally bring about appropriate outcomes.

'To let go...' what does that mean? Easy to say, not so easy to do!

The best way to begin letting go is to start with the things 'nearest to you'. No, that doesn't mean partners, friends and family. It means all those comforting little habits which arise but are not essential to happiness or easy living.

Here is a list you might begin with: Move the bed to the other side of the room; rearrange all of the cutlery in the drawer; shift all the plates and glasses to new positions; move the book shelves so that the big books are up high and the smaller ones below; shift the television (into the basement!); sit at a different place when you have breakfast, a different seat for dinner.

Because you are consciously agreeing to rearrange your environment, your habit-hungry mind is faced with waking up and actually looking at what you have been doing all this time. It gets the message.

Like this:

'Uh Huh, I never did like sitting with my back to the door when I'm on the telephone, Oh! And another thing, isn't it about time that squeaking door got fixed'. And so on.

This is why we can all do this so very happily…no cost, no pain!

Speaking of making change, I guess my mind got the better of me!

What happened to me after I greeted the idea of change so openly?

Life grabbed hold of me and convinced me that the appropriate change was to move boxes, chattels and family 2000 kilometres to Melbourne, Australia. Then the fun really began.

Soon after we arrived, I did a silly thing.

This was to go with a friend to the Melbourne Spiritualist church in A' Becket Street. Religion at that time held nothing for me. I'd given it a good try. As much younger men two of my friends and I had visited all the churches we could find, but when I couldn't find the answers I longed for, I gave up. So you see, in this case, I was just going along out of pure curiosity.

As we climbed the few steps a little old lady with a shock of white hair spied me.

Without the slightest hesitation she came directly over and said, 'You will be at Tulip's birthday party on Tuesday.'

To say that I was taken by surprise is an understatement! What could I say but, 'Tulip's birthday? Yes, yes, fine, right, Tuesday? OK?'

More than fifty people celebrated that evening. The party was for twelve-year-old Tulip, even though they explained that she had been burnt at the stake as a witch in Spain many centuries ago! Why she chose to hang around for the next few millennia helping people I didn't quite understand. But I was glad she did.

So. Can we really say this was all just an unusual coincidence?

That two different groups of people thousands of miles apart in different countries should believe in the same story? They all believed in Tulip. One used her for the benefit of their businesses and the other for confirming their spiritual beliefs.

Despite all that evidence, I was left with many questions.

I knew my own grandparents (whom I never met) with their 13 children, including my mother of course, held weekly seances, calling in spirits and following Spiritualist beliefs.

But my father was a strict pastor. Conflict upon conflict.

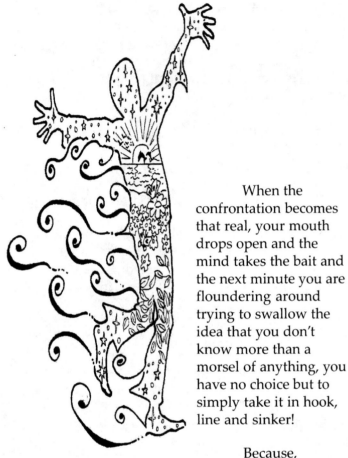

When the confrontation becomes that real, your mouth drops open and the mind takes the bait and the next minute you are floundering around trying to swallow the idea that you don't know more than a morsel of anything, you have no choice but to simply take it in hook, line and sinker!

Because, suddenly you have your feet on the ground. You wake up. Colours become intense.

Watching a golden daffodil opening in the spring becomes totally fascinating. To see a butterfly; to feel the joy of the migrating birds returning thousands of kilometres to their same nest; to marvel at the tiniest world in the microscope and the enormity of the unimaginable majesty of the universe. This is *freedom*.

If only we can do that, then all the questions about the reality of past lives, reincarnation, near death experiences and channelling wisdom through disembodied aliens from the stars dissolve away into the basket of uncertainty.

It no longer matters to you if there is a cosmic plan or whether the whole thing depends on coincidence.

<u>Flight 102: Flight Plan, Cockpit Check and debriefing</u>

READY TO FLY

1. Have your logbook at your side. A favourite pen at the ready?
2. Check that you are relaxed, comfortable. Mental seat belt clicked.
3. Headphones on the ears to hear the music of the spheres, or the commands from the higher self.
4. Plan exactly how long this flight will be. 20, 30, 50 minutes.
5. Set the clock.
6. Do not attempt to land any earlier.
7. Check the starting sequence – put your mind in focus before pressing the starter button (Check).
8. Check that there is no one and nothing to disturb your slow taxiing to the main runway (Check).
9. Prepare for take off. Turn into

wind. You are always clear to
proceed, ahead of all other traffic.
10. Lift the pen and begin writing.
11. Write the date and precise time.
12. What has happened since your
last flight?

....

13. Do you see that others, friends,
family, partners, have changed
towards you?

....

14. Are those day-dreamings still
sweet?

....

15. How are you doing with those
resistances? Write a long story
about the difficulty you have
accepting new ideas - but don't
stop even if you decide you are
the best person you know at
coping.

....

16. I don't want to....

....

17. I would love to....

....

18. Immediately the bell rings put
down your book, even if you are
in the middle of a sentence. It is
better to have an abrupt landing
than drift around aimlessly. Place
your logbook in your lap, close
your eyes and listen outwardly to
all the sounds around.

Play the *Mind Music* CD

grounding your thoughts.

Much later, long after you have returned to the tarmac of your surroundings, take out your logbook, read from the first entry to the last. Add anything that seems important *to you* especially any physical, emotional, spiritual and imagined changes.

5. The Mantra

Having a philosophy is not much use when the rent collectors are hammering at the door!

'Oh! Sorry, I just need to finish my daily conversation with the Star Beings and I'll be right with you - just pick up a cushion and contemplate the wellbeing of Californian orange trees for an hour or two!'

I don't think so.

To enjoy and nurture our own being we have to come to grips with disappointments, anger, suffering through delusions and illusions and all the imagined hurts we carry from cradle to grave... which is after all, reality! The Magic Life can only be achieved by diving into the mess which most of us call a 'mind'.

Unfortunately the unreconditioned mind is like a flock of swallows in the spring. Fluttering all over the sky, each one separately swooping, climbing, chasing tiny morsels on the wing. Individually the birds are desperately dedicated to renovating last year's nest ready for a brand new family. Each focusing on their own immediate needs. There is no collective melding.

Then as summer progresses the teenagers begin leaving home, they start flying solo for the first time.

Slowly the scattered minds of all the birds are drawn towards one intention.

As winter approaches they will fly the enormous distances from Stuttgart to Sydney, from Amsterdam to Adelaide, from Belgrade to Brisbane. In order to achieve this they must travel as one mind, interconnected and purposeful.

Just like those swallows in autumn, we are blessed with those zillions of thoughts; the trick for us is to teach them to fly in formation!

Because if you are going to fly half way round the world and you are no bigger than the palm of your hand, you need to focus *all* your intention and physical resources to do that.

And this brings us to one of the great paradoxes of a Magic Life.

Buckminster Fuller tells us that all of nature is subject to a phenomenon called 'precession' which means that the important action often happens at right angles (90 degrees) to the direction of the primary force.

To explain it we need to turn to the kingdom

(correctly the queendom) of the bees. The working bee spends his life focusing on gathering the nectar.

What he doesn't think about is that whilst putting his head into some pretty tricky situations to suck up the good stuff, he is, at the same time, dusting himself off with the pollen which sticks to his hindquarters. This in turn, means the flowers get fertilized, which means that everyone gets to have flowers next year and so on...

When we focus on a single idea of how to achieve our dreams we might get to the nectar but we are going to miss the importance of the pollen. It arrives at right angles to our desired path. We haven't left space for natural precession. When we keep a tight rein on our ambitions, cancelling all other options, we don't hear the phone call if it comes from a direction we are not expecting. When it does, and it always will, we usually question it with such cautious distrust that Nature becomes impatient with the waiting and She hangs up.

Truly, most of us are so conditioned we miss the magic of life, the enjoyment of seeing that whatever we simple mortals desire is always less than that which we are entitled to!

The same danger exists for us when we focus too tightly on what we want.

In order to avoid that, I recommend the use of a method which is thousands of years old. It allows us to free the mind from those zillions of loose thoughts without needing to travel 12,000 miles Down-Under, or even moving from the comfort of our lounge chairs. How fortunate!

In esoteric circles it is called reciting mantras. The mantra is a short saying, something like a condensed book for the lazy reader. Or maybe a handy way for the enlightened ones to talk to each other in shorthand.

Nothing is better to help you remember something important than repetition. Let's call it sublime brainwashing

It has nothing to do with religion.

Let's say you want to do this, you could start with one of the most famous of all mantras. The Tibetan *Om Mane Padme Hum* which is a perfect example of endless repetition of words creating a rhythm which, after a time, occupies the mind.

>> You are completely free to use the Tibetan words if you wish or, perhaps better still, at first, just pick any word, which ends with a vowel, it could even be your name. Sit quietly repeating it for half an hour or more.

You will notice that the *meaning* of the word becomes meaningless.

Do it out loud. Wow! Two powerful things happen. The mind is nicely coerced into trying to unravel whatever you are feeding it, and *at the same time*, you lose any idea of your own importance. How valuable is that?

One of my favourite mantras was being muttered over and over by a Buddhist monk who I was travelling with from Hongkong to Lhasa. For various reasons we had not eaten properly for two days. The final leg was a 90-kilometre drive from the airport to the city crowded into a 12-seater bus.

Sitting next to him I heard him repeating a mantra under his breath.

'What,' I said, feeling tired, hungry and a little irreverent 'is the mantra for today?'

With a huge smile he spoke louder, 'Om lunch. Om lunch. Om lunch.'

The mantra keeps our local mind occupied while life happens.

According to John Lennon, 'Life is what's happening while you are busy making other plans!'

It is not important to get hooked on the full, scientific explanation of the 'local mind'. For our purpose let's just say it is the bit of you that tells you that you are hungry, hot or cold, tired, angry, bored or a dozen other survival mechanisms which mostly happen without our conscious consent. You can say it has a mind of its own and it gets very upset when you ask it to shut up and let you get some peace and quiet.

The thing is we have to outflank the restless mind. We have to come at it from a different direction.

Like a spy in the night we must sneak in and give it something to divert its attention while we get down to the nitty-gritty of our wishes.

In the following chapters we will look at the use of mantras several times.

Meanwhile here is one which is not only good for the brain but also incredibly useful as a tool for overcoming insecurity, self-doubt and the feeling of always being unsuccessful. (It sounds remarkably like a prescription for one of the famous Bach Flower remedies!)

Here it is.

'I am doing the best that I can.' (In Italics!)

When I feel I have not done as well as I'd like, I mutter 'I am doing the best that I can' under my breath (so no one can hear me – I don't want them to think I am *totally* deranged!)

Regardless of whatever you call it, it will change your experience of daily life.

Here's another one to write down and practice:

Try, *'Isn't that interesting'*. See how immediately the effect can be used when you need to defuse an argument or you are puzzled why everything seems to be going wrong for unfortunate you.

'How interesting it is that I am angry with my best friend'.

'How interesting that my boss cannot see how valuable my work is to the company'.

During seminars I tell people they should regularly use this helpful method. In fact I have often said that I would like to have 'Isn't that interesting' carved on my tombstone.

6. The English Doctor

Here is what precession did for me.

Shortly after the memorable meeting with Tulip in Melbourne, I was accepted for a dream job. (Thanks Tulip!) It was the sort of position people would give their left arm for! (Or, if you are left-handed…oh, never mind…).

Senior Graphic Artist with GTV9, Australia's major commercial television network.

Those were the days, my friends. They were black and white days in more ways than one. Everything was new. It was long before destructive commercialism took over and we were more or less free to create whatever we could imagine.

We were standing in our own field of diamonds.

I can put an exact date to it because I was involved in the presentation of Neil Armstrong's moonwalk. For some months our department was preparing for it, as were the technical staff.

Few people realise that because of the moon's position at the time of his historic meanderings the entire broadcast was relayed through GTV9 in Melbourne to Houston.

You can be sure I was in the control room when it happened. This meant that, by a couple of microseconds, I was among the four other people in the *entire* world, who were first to see the man on the moon!!!

Yet being in television gave me more than I could ever have imagined. It gave me the opportunity to meet an unusual English doctor who was interviewed at the time by one of my colleagues.

Doctor Nell Holmes was not just any doctor. In the United Kingdom her natural ability to heal people and the successes she had with recalcitrant patients made her colleagues envious and suspicious. She was more or less forced to turn to the formal study of Spiritual Healing, coupled with numerology and it turned her own world upside down, literally, when she agreed to go to Tasmania and lecture on her work.

The reception was, I believe, overwhelming. In any case she chose to move to Melbourne, living in a delightful area surrounded by wild-flowers and sophisticated people.

Often, with my wife Dinah, and the two kids we would take a drive out to her 'ranch' and spend a pleasant Sunday afternoon.

We never once mentioned that my son, Craig (6), was born with a left eye with no vision. We had been told by several doctors that there were no nerve endings and there would never be any possibility of correction.

It wasn't that we didn't think of it but with such a diagnosis you have to put it in the back of your mind. Then, for some reason, which has never been very clear, one sunny day after Nell had brought out the biscuits and English tea, I said, 'Would you like to look at Craig's eye?'

As I write this I can still see her funny little smile. As though she had been keeping the chocolates from us.

'I can only help when someone *asks* for help,' she explained.

Then as the cicadas chirped and a couple of kangaroos loped past the open window, she took two fingers and rubbed them somewhere on the back of his skull.

'Ahh!' She said, 'there it is.'

A few moments pause then back to the conversation, tea and biscuits.

Next morning Craig came in and climbed into bed with us.

'Mum, Dad,' he said, 'I can see out of that eye'.

Is that a miracle or what?

He could now see shapes and colours in the 'blind' eye.

To say we were happy is an understatement.

The only disconcerting thing was that after helping Craig, Nell turned to me and said, 'you can do this. One day you will be doing this.'

Now, I can tell you very clearly, that is definitely not what I could possibly have imagined me doing. Under any circumstances.

It was OK for a trained doctor with years of medical and psychic training to do this thing. Me? Me! I had never dealt with anyone with a strained ankle let alone a real illness.

In those days it was considered very *avant-garde* to even think about healing. Visiting Nell was about as far as we would go. Certainly looking back there had been many occasions when the universe had done a back flip but had never directly confronted me with such an outrageous idea.

And then it did.

And I am sitting here in Germany 30 years later writing this book very well aware of the full impact she has had on my life. She *knew* anyone can do these things! No need for the guru trip! No need to become an outcast! Nothing more needed than a good cup of tea, a sunny room and a readiness to be of service to others.

Thanks Nell…wherever you are…here is one 'student' who is eternally grateful.

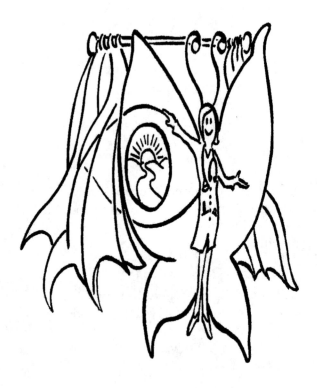

7. The Gift

New Zealand is, as a few of you know, about as far from anywhere else you can get - unless you live there and then it is the centre of your universe.

It is predominantly an agricultural country with just 4 million people and more than 80 million sheep. Some of us suspect that most of the politicians are actually reincarnated sheep!

For a small country we have almost every geographic feature found anywhere else in the world. It is like a pocket edition of the Traveller's Guide to the Universe.

It was New Zealanders who invented the bungee jump and aerial crop dusting. It was the first country to give women the vote and the first (the only one?) to declare an entire nation nuclear free.

And it gave the world Kiwi fruit!

The Maori of *Ao Tea Roa* (New Zealand) had the

'highest Neolithic culture the world has ever known.'[1] It was based on a complex social system.

They are renowned for their connection and respect for Nature.

Maori are the largest group of the Polynesians who have long been known as the navigators of the Pacific. Their territory takes in Hawaii, Tahiti, Cook Islands, Samoa and hundreds of atolls and islands.

According to Polynesian cosmology there is no separation between Time and Space.

Only just now modern physics is beginning to find ways to relate to this concept.

If we agree with this then it is true that all our ancestors and descendants are existing and experiencing the cosmos together with us right now.

I was lucky because my mother, long before she began writing, had been a nursing sister in a hospital in the centre of a rural area and was very familiar with the healing practices of Maori.

She didn't talk openly of it very often but there was always an undercurrent of comfort around these ideas.

Have you ever been given a present, perhaps for a birthday or at Christmas, and you are not quite sure which way to turn to say 'thank you' when you really do not need that thing?

I didn't know what to do with it. In fact I had no idea what it was!

It just, well…happened.

In fact it took me a long time to be comfortable with it.

Just to make it more difficult it is only in recent years that the possibility of a person directly affecting the stasis of another without physical intervention has been accepted.

Now, it is common knowledge.

But at that time the only way I knew something unusual was going on, was because many times people would ask me to help with their problems. On the rare occasions when I had a girl friend I would get frustrated because they would just want to *talk*!

Many times sick animals would come to me.

When you have this as a natural skill, no one taps you on the shoulder and says, 'Right, next semester, you study Healing 101, you only made a D grade in mathematics, so it's healing for you, start reading'.

In most Western cultures the idea of a person being able to directly change the health of another is still seldom accepted. The notable exception is the Catholic Church.

It came as a surprise when Father Ron Lindgren, the media spokesperson for the Catholic

Church of USA, interviewing me on radio said, in answer to a sceptical caller, 'We cannot be hypercritical, because for many centuries the church has acknowledged miraculous healings. We have always recognised that some people have the ability to make spiritual and physical change for a suffering person.'

The record shows that most of the people who have been declared saints were canonised because of their demonstration of healing ability.

Fortunately in the 21st century the healer is no longer at risk of torture and excommunication - as he was before, unless he was a priest.

Leo Tolstoy, the famous Russian writer, was excommunicated because he dared to write a book in 1895, titled *'The Kingdom of God is Within You'* which in modern language translates as that each of us is inherently a saint, a healer, a hero.

The first book I read from cover to cover was Tolstoy's *'War and Peace'*, which my eldest brother Ralph had brought home hoping to read it before I grabbed it and devoured it! Somehow the story made me fascinated with Tolstoy's Russia. Never imagining that one day I would spend so much of my time there. (I have even had the incredible opportunity to sit in the chair he used when writing his books and to visit his unmarked grave in the forest he so loved).

Constant reading heightened my strong wish to travel, little realising that, as Kahili King (*Urban Shaman*) explains, there are two types of gaining the knowledge by Polynesian healers - *tohunga*, Maori and *kahuna,* Hawaiian.

One way is by sitting at the feet of a teacher...much the same as the guru/student relationships of India.

The other gains the knowledge by travelling endlessly, financially supported (more or less!) by his or her skill at offering service to other people. Meeting and hearing dozens of teachers without being devoted to any single one.

Could this apply to me? Could it be that I am the Navigator?! A traveller comfortable in any realm?!

I am not going to pretend that one morning 'God' spoke to me and I woke up with dancing hands and a permanently incandescent halo, my spirit emanating unconditional love and peace all over the place.

Sorry, what a good story that would have made! But the truth is I still rejected the thought out of hand.

And it took a lot of work to overcome the confusion and disruption created by the absolutely outrageously unique events.

Certainly for many years I never imagined that my ability would be measured in the world of science and medicine.

As it was for me, so it is for most of us, there is a special moment in our lives when we have the chance to sit down and, by recalling odd or unexplained things, we see a glimpse of the path laid out for each of us.

If we know how to look for them, we do see extraordinary things happening even in the most mundane moments.

What arose for me were a number of things which definitely did not fit into the world of advertising or common sense. Wherever I turned the Field gave me a gentle kick in the backside to get me moving on the path I had come here for. And I proved to be a slow learner!

I can justify some of that. I chose a father who was a dedicated Methodist minister. I respected his views but as a child I could not sit still through his sermons without asking, or more accurately, thinking, endless questions.

On the rear wall of our tiny wooden church, there were fake laurel leaves 50 cms high spelling out just three words. They proclaimed 'God Is Love'. Now here is the conundrum. My childish thoughts ran, Is God Love? Or, equally, Love is God! Perhaps even God Love Is.

I chewed it over for a decade or so sitting watching those leaves get more and more faded and dusty until the time came when I was old enough to say, 'enough'.

My Conclusion…God Love *Is*.

If God Love exists then we should be able to experience it.

She doesn't expect you to just believe. After all

belief is no more than something you feel to be true. Faith is something that someone else asks you to believe because they do.

Both are like trees without roots – a lot of leafy dressing but no support.

Your mind can't help forever dancing with the awkward feeling that there is something missing.

At worst you chastise yourself for being a criminally insane unbeliever, at best you put on a smiling face and wish to heaven you didn't need to fake it.

The reason I am writing this book is that I am sure we can all find a way to discover our own healing ability. If it can happen to me, it can happen to you. *You can heal your family, your friends and with a little training, discover your life's purpose through service to others.* I just want to share with you how to get there.

8. Being Spiritual – Spiritual Being

The first thing to avoid is trying too hard to be 'spiritual'. It might be just wasting an entire life because you are on a round trip anyway. Every one of us, at birth, is automatically issued with a pre-stamped Return Ticket Home (no visa required). There are no concessions. Spiritual is what you were before you arrived and spiritual is what you will return to.

Meanwhile. Get on with it.

I heard a delightful story when I was in Boston. It was about a family with two children. The oldest, Jennifer, was 4 years old, her sister 3 months. One evening the parents were sitting quietly reading. Through the baby minding system they could hear Jennifer go into the baby's room. Leaning closely, she whispered to her sister, 'can you tell me what God is like. I am starting to forget.'

That's the plan.

Here is an announcement! You have won the greatest lottery of all time. The Big One. If your mum or dad hadn't sneezed at the appropriate moment, it would be your brother or sister reading this book.

Here is what you have won.

A chance to have a go at living in the physical world.

Here are the game rules.

1): You are not to know why you won the number one ticket.

2): You will never be sure if you are playing correctly.

3): Everyone around you has no idea who you *really* are, or why you keep bumping up against their portion of the prize.

4): As soon as you think you know what's going on, the ground shifts and you are transported back to square one.

5): People who are exactly as lost as you, will console themselves by trying hard to make you lose the game.

And if that's not enough, you have been dumped into the middle of a human culture which shows no consideration for the place where you are living, for the other beings who are sharing the ride, or Nature herself.

It doesn't look like you've won much of a prize!

But here you definitely are.

If you don't know why you are alive. There is a simple answer.

Write this down...

We are here to learn how to be of service to others.

That is not too difficult a task.

Not only that, your *return to joy* depends on it.

Have you ever met someone who always seems to be depressed? Maybe a friend or a partner? A person you know quite well?

Their depression is caused by having no focus in their lives. Isn't that true?

In almost all cases it is the lack of purpose which causes their depression. The missing link to their wholeness.

There are only two things we can be sure of in life.

One is: I am here and alive.

The second is that every sentient being (you are one of those) will one day die.

All else is speculation and delusion.

Wow! Doesn't that make you feel insecure!?

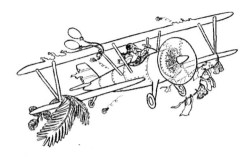

Flight 103: Flight Plan, Cockpit Check and debriefing

CHANGES TO PLANS

1. Have your logbook at your side. A favourite pen at the ready?
2. Check that you are relaxed, comfortable. Mental seat belt clicked.
3. Headphones on the ears to hear the music of the spheres, or the commands from the higher self.
4. Pre-flight check. Read back what you have written between flights. Keep writing whenever the mood takes you. Deliberately spend time looking back, relating past memories.
5. Take up the pen. Write the exact date and time.
6. Just as you line up for take-off. the interfering busy bodies in the control tower tell you that your entire plan is not accepted.
7. What do you do?
8. In that flash of a moment your entire life has been changed. How can you cope with that?

9. Write down what you have done
   in similar cases. Keep writing.
   Think of, and write down (fully)
   what you have done when it is
   not your choice to make
   changes. Be honest.
10. In retrospect, how many of those
    turned out to your benefit?
11. Commit yourself to a list of
    changes you could 'play' with
    without cost or drama.

Place your logbook in your lap, close your eyes
and listen outwardly to all the sounds around,
grounding your thoughts.

Deeply residing
within each living
cell is the
ancient memory
of the most
powerful
force in the Universe
- the will to survive

●

Ignorance alone
stands in the way of
realising that joy

9. The Healer?

Forgive me if I confound you, but whenever I write or think that word 'healer?' I always want to put a question mark at the end of the word.

It has been so misused and misrepresented in all sorts of situations that it no longer means what it intends to represent.

We will need to find agreement that we are all talking about the same thing.

Once there was a man who really, *really* loved chocolate. Can you imagine how happy he was when he got a dream job in a chocolate factory? On his second day at work he was smelling the hot chocolate cooking in a huge vat. AAH! ... The smell! OOOH! ... The colour....mmmm!

Maybe, he thought, 'I could just taste a little bit if I just leant forward a little more'. Then tragedy, his foot slipped and - gloooop - he fell right into the thick, black mass.

Scared for his life he started shouting, 'Fire!

Fire!'

His co-workers, rushing up, hauled him out and asked, 'Where is the fire, we didn't see any fire?'

He replied, 'would you have come and saved me if I had started shouting, 'Chocolate! Chocolate!'?

So if we are forced by the language of communication to say 'healing' instead of 'chocolate' at least within this book, we will know we mean something different to, well, healing?

Healing? We have to be very careful before we use that word.

When it comes to the practice of 'healing?' We are faced with huge questions. On every side there are healers?

Throughout history there have been shamans, witchdoctors, medicine men, magi and a dozen other assorted types but for them to be acknowledged within their own communities, they needed a lifetime of study and inherited right.

It has become very fashionable and prestigious to call yourself a 'healer'. Having such a title has become glamorous but very few people realise that along with that comes a completely different way of living, with all the accompanying responsibilities.

It is the time for us to truly know that nature has already provided us with the program for self-regenerating. And within that surety we can completely relax, giving ourselves over to the service of others.

The difficulty which most people see in this approach is that it seems to be too *simple*.

Even if we accept that, there is still a lot of courage needed to transform the rational education most of us have suffered under.

At the beginning we can get a lot of comfort from adopting the new philosophy but it only becomes useful if we allow it to become our way of life.

Fortunately the new way is so clear and supportive that we soon wonder why on earth we didn't hear about this long before we made all those silly 'mistakes' in our decisions and choices.

For me, even though my world expanded exponentially, it was still more of an interruption than a serious change of plan. For years I never considered taking it beyond reading books such as '*Jonathan Livingston Seagull*', Lobsang Rampa books, the seminal book - '*Psychic Discoveries Behind the Iron Curtain*' – an echo of my subdued interest in things Russian.

Meanwhile, I produced advertising campaigns; a weekly film and theatre review for a major newspaper, lectured at a film and television school and was thoroughly hooked on the adrenaline of meeting deadlines and creating scripts for films.

No, no, there wasn't a flash of lightning, but one morning as I sat to write an urgent television advertisement, it was as though the switch had been thrown. There was no doubt. I just couldn't write any more. The rhythm of the keyboard had lost its fascination.

I knew then it was time to sell everything and, like the *'Carpet Baggers'* of Steinbeck's story, put a few possessions in the car and drive the 2000 miles from Perth to Sydney.

Destination and destiny entirely unknown.

This is worth remembering. When we unhook ourselves from the deep ruts we have carved from fear of letting go, all hell breaks loose!

For the first time in my life, I ran out of money and ended up being asked, not politely, to get out of the flat I had rented. Living in my car the funny thing was, I had kept this super fancy automobile and here I was, penniless, sitting with the dog on the roadside contemplating my fate. Of course I questioned God about this. But in a slightly different intonation than Neale Donald Walsch might have used!

Next week, I went to the public baths, washed the dust from my hair and applied for a job. I was immediately offered the job as resident director of a film company, travelling first class up and down the country, checking potential clients and hosting important business lunches.

That lasted long enough for me to re-establish a place to live, then the old feeling came back.

I said to myself, 'Hey! I am a first class *traveller*! I need to move on'.

You have to understand that at that time in Australia there was a government, bless them, who were new to the job and got carried away with their personal interest in support of the arts.

Those of us who felt comfortable declaring ourselves creative professionals, discovered what we euphemistically called, 'the unofficial grant'.

In other societies you might call it, 'social support', 'the dole' or 'unemployment payments' but we needed this indirect income to give us some space to develop new ideas. It worked marvellously well. Most of the Australian films of that era were written and directed with the help of that unofficial grant.

It didn't matter that I would end the week with 20 cents in the pocket. I had the incredible freedom to spend the days getting back to my writing and riding untold kilometres on my favourite bicycle!

Soon enough I turned to different life styles... as if there weren't enough changes already in my life!

10. Piloting the Ship - The Cosmic Plan

Although I very easily remembered Nell's words, I went many years without doing anything about it. Running my advertising and film making business took seven-days-a-week focus.

At that time in most countries the only people who were regularly practicing what they termed 'Spiritual Healing' were members of the Spiritualist Churches. That felt better. I attended one or two services.

At those meetings I didn't notice being noticed.

But after a few visits one of the young ladies I hardly knew asked me if I would offer her healing.

She told me that her thyroid was not working and she was due to have it removed surgically next week. Phew! I had no idea what was a thyroid. I still don't. But in my naïve ignorance I thought that if the thing wasn't working and wasn't going to go rotten and begin smelling, why not leave it there?

Anyway, because of her anxiety we agreed to meet at my place the next day. That didn't give me time to back out.

Before she arrived, I arranged an ordinary straight-backed kitchen chair for her to sit on in the middle of my lounge room, (I was too embarrassed to suggest she lie down which would have been much more comfortable for her).

So I asked her to close her eyes (I knew that part of the drill) and sort of waved my arms around, cleaning her aura... I thought.

I stepped back waiting for a gasp of gratitude. She didn't move. She didn't move for a minute. She didn't move for 10 minutes. Is this how healing goes? I didn't have any training, no teacher to call. All I had done was shake my hands at her.

I began to panic. She seemed to be in some sort of coma. Maybe a trance. Don't touch her, my mind told me.

Should I call an ambulance? What if they came? What should I tell them?

'This lady, who I don't know, walked in, sat down and went into this fit.'

If medical science says it is impossible to affect someone in this way, can they hold me responsible for this tragedy?

For far too long she stayed that way, then as

though jolted with an electric shock she snapped her eyes open.

'Thank you sooooo much,' she said ' I feel so gooooood'.

I didn't.

I quickly guided her out of the door before any reaction could set in. If she was going to do that again it was not going to be on my time!

More than a little shaken (I didn't feel I should ask for a fee at that time!), I instantly decided my healing career was to follow my film career and that lady's thyroid. Surgically removed without protest!

Most of the next week I sort of hid out like an outlaw in fear of the posse breaking in and dragging me off to the nearest lynching tree.

Then the phone call came. It was her. Panic again.

How sweet she sounded. 'The surgeon did a final test before the operation,' she bubbled, 'he thinks there must have been a misdiagnosis because my thyroid is working even better than expected for a normal 32-year-old woman.'

Back to the drawing board as we used to say. Start afresh!

I breathed a huge sigh of relief and gratefulness not only to her, for her intuitive choice to try my beginner's mind, but just out into space and the unknowable Universe.

So what can we learn from that story?

What cannot be denied is this: if the principle has ever worked, it must operate within an immutable law of nature. As certain as gravity, it cannot be turned on or off depending on the whim of the student. Or the skill of the operator.

In my case, I'd had no real training - just a wish to help a person in trouble.

>> In a state of not knowing what I was doing, something dramatic had happened.

Quite casually I had used a phrase which later became very important to me whenever I am asked to help, I say, 'let *us* see what *we* can do?' The emphasis is on the 'we'. This quite rightly removes the ego of the 'healer' and at the same time invites the 'patient' to share in the responsibility of their own improvement. Most importantly, it brings the experience into a tangible reality, neatly taking away the expectation of a one-shot miracle from a 'miraculous' healer.

Once I had recovered from my week of torment I tentatively agreed when others came to see me seeking their own 'thyroid story'. Not just physical concerns. Emotional worries and upsets, and relationships.

Slowly I became quite busy, no longer needing the government's unknowing help.

Soon, as we say 'out of the blue', unexpectedly I was invited to come and meet the people who were establishing the Sydney Cancer Information and Support Group.

Now, that was a big jump for me. I had never met anyone with cancer. How do they look?

Are they able to talk, walk, eat? Anything?

I had not yet understood that true healing doesn't separate illnesses into the 'tough ones' or into the 'easy' baskets. Keep this in mind. Cancer is presented as a worse illness than others because medical science has such difficulty with it. Are you ready for this? Here comes another of those synchronicities.

The very first day I went to Hunter's Hill to meet the group, I walked in behind a man who was holding a prescription form from the Bristol Cancer Clinic (U.K.) which advised him to have healing once a week for his inoperable brain tumour.

The receptionist told him the Support Group did not know of a healer. With a little embarrassed cough I stepped a little closer and suggested that I just might be able to help.

Before we go on with David's amazing story, I want to diverge a little and explain that **'healing' is the natural extension of our own compassion for others**.

There is no need to think of it as something only a few gifted ones can do. This whole book is to show you that, even if you do not decide to devote your life to this work, there are plenty of things you can do to make your life sooooo much happier just by connecting with the most natural of all states. The one of being healthy.

If we are alive, we are healers of some sort or other. We are born that way. Your DNA insists on it!

We should *all* begin the day by repeating to ourselves 'khoroshooor...khoorooshooor...'

As I tell David's story what we are going to have to accept, is that this is one example of what is possible *all of the time.*

I am sure for David it was more out of desperation than being impressed by me, but he had little option left.

His wife, Barbara, was even less impressed. 'You are going to drive 80 kilometres twice a week to see a *freak*! You must be crazy!'

Nevertheless he came three, then four times.

On the fifth visit his wife came too. I assumed it was to give me the rounds of the kitchen!

He sat quietly with a glum look on his face. Then staring me in the eye he said, 'well Clif, I had a CAT scan two days ago'.... dramatic pause.... 'the doctors said there is no tumour'.

They both fell about laughing. I had a tear in my eye for sure.

He was not a young man and he died almost a year later of pneumonia. I would love to say he caught it skiing but you already know that there is not so much snow in Australia!

That happened 24 years ago and Barbara, who became a good friend, remarried and ever since has kept in touch, usually by email.

I cannot say that my work was all clear sailing for me. For a while I was caught on the waves of 'Spiritual Healing', and I embraced those ideas.

No doubt it is very effective but I just couldn't *feel* those elusive guardian spirits around me as I worked.

Knowing of Tulip was very comforting, yet there was a gap between the educated mind and the reality of watching these mind-blowing events.

But somewhere in the Field of Information, without my conscious agreement, the exact learning curve I needed and could cope with, unfolded for me.

Not by chance (isn't that a lovely, totally correct

phrase), I was introduced to the social worker at St. George's Oncological hospital, Sydney's largest. He arranged lectures for me and each fortnight I would come to the hospital's support group and fix up a few tears and troubles.

From that connection I was asked if I would visit a very sick man who couldn't leave his house.

Following the method which had been showing such success I had him lie down and I sat behind his head and switched on as much attention as I could muster. Nothing happened.

Pour on more energy, I told myself. Nothing.

Suddenly a terrible thought came to my mind. So much of the work is voluntary that I was always very low on money. It occurred to me that in my haste to run in to see him I had parked in a twenty-minute zone. That could be a fifty dollar fine.

Can you see the picture? I am unable to move! I must stay with this man for long enough to complete my idea of what he needs.

Go or stay? Go or stay?

Then, under my hands he sort of shuddered.

'What happened then,' he said, almost shouting, 'that was so hot, so powerful.'

I felt like shouting back...I got it! I got it! As soon as I had taken my little mind out of the way and focused on *my* problem, the flaming torch hit!

If you truly understand what had happened, you can close the book right now. Because all the rest is about the path of letting go and allowing the incredible Universe pilot the plane.

Wait a minute! Wait a minute! I didn't really *mean* that!

We are launched into a remarkable journey together. Please don't desert the ship (leap out of the plane) mid passage.

Imagine how fear-less our life would become if we saw it as a ship travelling, say from London to New York. There is a captain and crew who have done the trip hundreds of times and are completely competent, so we do not need to concern ourselves about that.

The ship will travel from London to New York according to her sailing schedule. Meanwhile we can dance, play the poker machines, have kids, arguments and lovers and all the myriad things which are available in a human life. Then the ship docks in New York.

Before you know it, it's time to disembark, hopefully carrying as little accumulated junk as possible.

Before we go overboard with all these deep and serious thoughts, here is another lesson provided by the world at large. It is about a monk in Burma.

11. The Burmese Monk

The time came when I had separated from my wife and that was a painful and confusing exercise of letting go. Once again I had to allow things in my life to take their own shape.

Being alone, I had the space to investigate the old question of the concept of free will. This idea is usually clung to by people who have a deep fear of losing control - as if we ever had that.

Some of us think the best thing to do with all that academic stuff is to say this: If there is free will, then I will choose, through my free will, to give it up! How simple it is after all to discover freedom from the mind.

Why are we here? What is the purpose of my life? I still could not get the answers from the Christian church but I was hesitant to dive into other philosophies - expecting the same walls of rejection to questioning. As if to question was to immediately declare disbelief.

Can you imagine then, how I felt when a friend took me to a Buddhist temple in Sydney? I took one look at all those golden Buddhas. Pagan idols! I assumed, and I took off as fast as Lance Armstrong on the Tour de France!

The trouble was that I like getting my fingers burnt. The more I am told I am on the wrong track, the deeper I dig in my heels and hold on for the danger of it all.

I started sneaking into 'forbidden' temples and Buddhist lectures. Even reading books with titles like 'As The Buddha Said'.

Next came ten-day silent retreats far out in the Australian bush at a magic Thai Wat (forest monastery).

If you ever want to scare the daylights out of yourself go and sit through the night in the Australian bush.

Grown men cry!

Unlike tropical jungles or the African savannah, the bush sleeps quietly through the day, and then as evening comes and night falls, there are unexplainable noises which are not natural to the untrained ear.

What happens is this. As the temperature drops, huge chunks of eucalyptus tree bark break off and fall through the dry branches, shattering the silence of the night.

You are definitely going to need the Buddhist

technique of overcoming the illusion of fear by sitting imagining the tiger's breath as he crunches into your skull. Some people who are not familiar with tigers may choose to imagine the same effect happens with the dentist's drill.

It is a little more real when you are sitting in the middle of a dark forest full of poisonous snakes, marauding wombats, wild dingoes and sexually overactive kangaroos.

Surviving sane from those days gives us great training in calmness in the face of angry employers, tax inspectors, bureaucrats and, if you need it, snakes, crocodiles and black-widow spiders.

An opportunity arose to visit Burma. At that time you could only get a seven-day visa and so I went into 'tourist mode'; a quick trip up to Mandalay; a horse cart ride around the pagodas in Pagan and the mandatory visit to the Shwedagon (look it up!).

If I were asked to write the Concise Book of Burma as I experienced it, even after one short visit, it would fill a volume. Wonderful people, incredible history, immense statues, terrible railways!

Towards the end of my stay I was walking through the crowded streets of Rangoon. It is a fact that most Europeans are taller than Asians. Which means, as a European, as I walked through the teeming streets most of what I saw was a sea of bobbing black heads.

The crush of people every day is like the mob leaving a football stadium after the final match of the season. Your attention has to be more on where you are stepping than on the surroundings.

One day, walking along, suddenly I could feel my head was turning to one side. It was a strange feeling, unlike anything I had felt before. Just as though the muscles on the right side of my neck were constricting.

I resisted the movement.

Three of four more steps and it came again.

I was not going to give in to it.

This time more urgent, more insistent.

I gave in to the pressure.

My eyes followed the source of this puzzle to the other side of the untidy street and caught on the face of a thin, bearded man who was staring at me.

He looked perfectly normal apart from that wispy beard (Burmese men do not have beards) and his sarong (*longe*) was quite conventional if longer and plainer than others, which made me think he must be a monk.

As our eyes met, in my head I heard a sound

like a jumbo jet taking off.

The impact was dramatic. I stumbled a little, looking down to avoid stepping on someone. Within a glance I looked back and he was not there.

The strangest thing of all was that it felt so incredibly *normal*. The truth is I just had a feeling of warmth inside. No ringing in the ears, no sudden revelation, nothing more than a step missed as I walked.

Much later I became sure that what he did was to download all his wisdom into my consciousness. From then on, when people asked me all sorts of philosophical questions, I found I could answer them without hesitation. Even things I had never read of or studied.

It was he who did it; I was not looking for him. You understand, I don't suggest you take a flight to Burma tomorrow. He probably isn't there any more, if he ever was.

You could say my greatest teacher never was!

The word we are looking for here is transmission.

It is nonverbal communication practised not only by skilled teachers, but in its simplest forms by every one of us. That's the way I have learnt to teach my students.

It's the 'uh huh' experience – you are listening intently to a complicated explanation by a teacher or a friend and in one instant you comprehend it. Uh huh.

Put it this way. We are all bombarded by human generated 'radio' beams. To tune the antenna all that is needed is a little training, an open mind and a great deal of easy-going humour. With laughter you can defuse the static created by the sceptical mind and then reception is better than the BBC on a good-weather day.

If transmission is a little cloudy for you, then begin by thinking in terms of that which is known (by me) as *contagious proximity*. Our emotional state will be *transmitted* non-verbally to any person who is nearby.

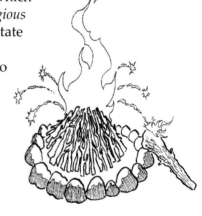

Without doubt we have all experienced it. If someone nearby yawns, whether we are tired or not, we 'join' them.

Professional comedians know it very well. To get the audience laughing they begin by focusing on one person in the audience. They tell that first joke directly to that person who laughs out of polite embarrassment, whether they get the joke or not. The rest of us join in.

v Try this. Next time your partner or a working colleague is angry, upset or argumentative, stop and look at how it affects your own mood. Isn't that interesting?

If I am calm, you will become calm. If upset, you will feel the same.

The Burmese monk was using the same principle, admittedly far in advance of the sleepy yawner! In everyday life you can use this. It is the same basic realisation we use to help others as 'healers'.

As long as we do not allow ourselves to be mind-lessly affected by surroundings and other's negative emotions, we can broadcast help to others without a word passing our lips. Do not believe or disbelieve until you try. Only polite emails will be answered!

Of course just as anything worthwhile takes some training to get 'professionally' comfortable, so it is the same with this. You can start now.

The conundrum is: how did the monk know I would be ready to receive what he was offering? How was it that I was right there at the right moment?

Zen people tell us that when the student is ready the teacher appears. What they never told me was that sometimes the teacher might bodily disappear before my very eyes!

Did I warn you that we might get into some strange magic in this book together?

Oh! And another thing. I am not sure I have emphasised enough that if anything has ever happened anywhere in the Universe once, it has to be one of the immutable laws of nature. Did I tell you that? Some things, such as two and two equals four, are the same whether you are in the Amazon jungle or floating in a space ship near Mars.

The second law is that if anyone can do it, we can *all* do it. We can use it for friends, family, pets and the struggling ozone layer.

For disbelievers who insist on 'keeping their feet on the ground', there is only boredom, cold weather and paralysis of the mind.

For those of us who know that above the clouds the sun is *always* shining, there are no glum days.

12. The Field

The broadcast of emotions and moods is happening around us at all times. We live in the centre of something which we can call a Field.

It is also known as: The Universal Field, The Field of Information, The Information Field Of Creativity, The Zero Point Field, the Quantum Field, The Akasha Field, The Morphogenetic Field, The Energy Field. *Ad infinitum.*

It has been known to Chinese and Hindus for thousands of years and they believe you cannot explain it because as soon as you attempt to explain it, it ceases to have meaning.

I like to call it The

THE FIELD

Information Field of Creativity because in such way we are all co-creating our own reality - whether we know it or not!

The Field permeates our thoughts, our bodies, our pains and our feelings of disconnectedness. It forms the galaxies and at the same time, the tiniest flexing of your intentions.

It breathes into our lives, and it creates the illusion of material substance.

Even though it is impossible to *describe* the Field, we are subject to its laws. And the main law is that when a particle changes its whereabouts, the entire Universe has to reshuffle the cards. Not only that, our bodies are a rather large collection of particles and we are affected whether we recognise it or not, by the cycles of the moon, by magnetic storms and many other natural forces.

The most well known example of this are the solar explosions of the sun which are frequently followed by wars, epidemics and social unrest. Human beings also affect nature much more than most realise.

In a personal 1983 interview, Professor Geoffrey Goodman of Tucson University told me that he had been considered a maverick and perhaps had even astonished himself and definitely his colleagues when his PhD thesis was accepted. He showed that in the wide river valleys of North America the water table fell whenever a tribe became warlike, forcing them to move on to find new pastures. A clear correlation between the warrior attitude and the surrounding nature. What sort of parable should our militaristic present leaders of the world pay attention to?

Clearly they do not understand that *everything* is interdependent and interconnected so that if a butterfly flaps its wings in China the tides in Norway will change.

But nothing is new!

These very facts were written into the Bible. We are told that should even one tiny sparrow fall from the sky, God makes a note of it. I do not really think He/She wanders around checking the aviary population.

For one thing He is kept busy holding up the ceiling of the Sistine chapel in the Vatican.

Science, with a great struggle, has had to come to agree with the viewpoint of the ancient sages.

As physicist David Bohm put it:

'We are all connected and operate within living Fields of thought and perception. The world is not fixed but is in constant flux; accordingly, the future is not fixed, and so can be shaped. The question to be resolved: how to remove the blocks and tap into that knowledge in order to create the kind of future we all want?'

Still it is difficult to explain what the living Field really is. It is as impossible as describing water to a fish, air to a bird or life to a human.

The Field of Creativity has no boundaries; it spreads across the Universe like a warm breath.

C'MON MATE! LET'S HAVE SOME FUN
AND RESHUFFLE THE UNIVERSE A BIT!

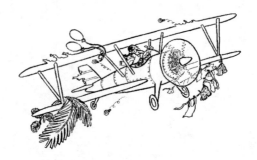

Flight 104: Flight Plan, Cockpit Check and debriefing

STALLS

1. Have your logbook at your side. A favourite pen at the ready?
2. Check that you are relaxed, comfortable. Mental seat belt clicked.
3. Headphones on the ears to hear the music of the spheres, or the commands from the higher self.
4. Review the last entries in your logbook.
5. Do you agree with what you wrote then? Expect not to!
6. Check you will not be disturbed. For goodness sake *turn off* the television! (Check).
7. Check that you are not waiting to rush off to another appointment (Check).
8. Lift the pen and write the exact date and time.
9. Without the slightest hesitation

start writing. Stalling is dangerous. One of the very first skills to learn when flying is to avoid stalling. Trying to reach for the sky too quickly without enough power brings your plane to a dead stop midair. Nose high in the air, tail facing the ground. Silence.

10. Stalling when trying for enlightenment is equally dangerous. Start at where you feel best... 'I am doing the best that I can'. But, without starting the engine, you are stranded half way there into the air, half way down into the hopeless pits.

11. Recovering from the stall, point the nose at the ground and wait until the air-speed picks up and the plane comes into control. Safe. Another tick in the record of your logbook.

Place your logbook in your lap, close your eyes and listen outwardly to all the sounds around grounding your thoughts.

13. Plants and Animals do it

Here are some fundamental stories which are quite different yet reinforce the interconnectedness of each of us and the world around us.

These are all expressions of the great desire of life to continue and we are coming to see that plants are not exempt from this enveloping Field, creating their own mechanisms of protection and procreation.

Professor Wouter van Hoven, a physiologist at the University of Pretoria, South Africa, was asked to investigate the puzzling deaths of gazelles in fenced off, protected areas.

There were no predators, no obvious diseases, just a withering away from malnutrition.

The first breakthrough came when it was discovered that their intestines were all tanned. Just as leather becomes tough and hard, they could not get any nutrition.

Where did the tannin come from?

After some brilliant detective work he found that when animals graze on trees there is a 44 percent increase of tannin in the leaves within 15 minutes; after one hour it increases by up to 282 percent. The explanation is that while animals in the wild are able to move on and forage somewhere else where the food is still tasty, the protected gazelles in the confines of the sanctuary were forced to eat leaves with high tannin content. Thus the tanned stomachs.

That is interesting enough, but listen. Trees up to *one kilometre away*, at the time of impact of the grazing animals, would also, almost at the speed of thought, increase their tannin content, their consciousness expanding, as the work of David Rhoades has shown, to include other plants in the vicinity which also react *whether they had been attacked or not.*

If plants live within such an evolved communication network then it may not be too difficult to accept their ability to foresee events which appear random to our 'educated' minds.

Do you see the implication?

Here is a very practical demonstration of the Field In Action (note the capital letters!).

Rats do it too! I was in Moscow at the time when Yeltsin was attempting to unseat Gorbachev. What interested me was that three days before the putsch, rats were seen during daylight running in the streets of Moscow and other Russian cities. They must have known ahead of time that there would be no danger to them during the unrest.

If animals can do it, so can you. You *are* one.

Observing nature has never been more rewarding.

Survival: Nature's need.

Let's go back to look at some other rats… in the 1920's researcher William McDougal of Harvard University, studied the abilities of rats to correctly solve mazes. He found that children of rats that had learned the maze, were able to run it faster — at first the rats would get it wrong 165 times before being able to run it perfectly each time, but after a few generations it was down to 20.

Rupert Sheldrake[2] felt that this was evidence of a morphogenetic Field. The rats running the maze the first time built their pattern of learning into the 'rat Field', and later rats were able to draw on this patterning.

Then, and this is exactly what I am saying about the Field of Information, not only rats all over the world could do the same, but even ones who had not been born until after the oldies died, could do the same.

14. Bees do it too

Arthur Koestler was reported to have observed a scientific experiment to discover how bees tell each other which direction to fly for the best nectar. When loaded bees return to the hive, they tell their colleagues which direction is the nectar by doing a dance on the threshold of the hive. Curious scientists decided that each morning they would meet at nine in the morning and decide where to move the hive that day and video the difference in the dance. The beekeeper, presumably more interested in bees than science, noticed that a full half-hour before the

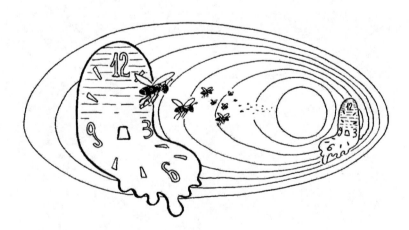

scientists decided where to move the hive, the bees were already waiting at that location.

What I like about these stories is that they do not depend on belief or fantasy. In most cases they either have solid data behind them or the phenomenon has been repeated over centuries.

In one of my earlier books, *'Dancers in the Fields'* I told of meeting a doctor from Southern India.

He said that where he came from, if a mango tree was not bearing much fruit, the people would get an elephant to violently shake it. Next year - lots of fruit.

Was it just a folk tale or could it be confirmed with some practical research?

In most of the world elephants are now a little scarce. But there is nowhere that does not have regular earthquakes.

Would it be possible to demonstrate that crop rates vary depending on the extensiveness of earth tremors?

I turned to the parts of the world where the most subterranean activity takes place – Japan, California and New Zealand, (a sort of giant example of the gazelles brunching on the trees – or maybe elephant stampedes)?

I am no statistician but as far as I can see for California[3], through 1955-1980 the years when there was an increase in the number and strength of earthquakes, there were significant increases in orchard crops. The same appeared to be the case with peaches in Japan.

You know what we are doing? We are looking for probable repetitions of observed phenomena. Which means that the Field is not so far away as we imagine.

And what about us, the humanity bunch?

Taking the average birth rate comparing California with the rest of the United States, the line rises above the average each year of increased or larger tremors.

The same applies in New Zealand.

In nature there are endless examples of the Field-in-Action.

Red Admiral butterflies in Canada wake up one morning late in summer, pack their tiny luggage and head south. By the time their great-great-great-grand children return next spring there have been many generations who have enjoyed the Mexican sunshine. Year after year the Field unerringly guides their offspring on the long journey without so much as a road map, much less a geographical positioning system!

Just a minute. It is not so difficult to imagine this happening with large animals and birds. Geese, for example migrate thousands of miles. They have a large brain capacity. They probably have some sort of chemico-electromagnetic radar which is taught directly to tot from mum. Whereas the butterfly must access the collective mind to be able to pass on the information, 'left turn at Colorado, veer right to avoid the Great Lakes'.

The world's largest living organism is the Great Barrier Reef off the northeast coast of Queensland, Australia. On the full moon evening each November all of the coral spoors, hundreds of kilometres apart, all at once rise to the surface to be fertilised. How do they know when their partners are ready to dance?

The thing is, all this tells us that we are not alone! Humans are just as integrated into the Field as the loneliest dung beetle.

15. The Hawaiian Dolphins

Living with the Field creates such a blessing, that when you open your heart, joy returns.

Along with that immeasurable happiness comes the responsibility which you have inherited. Therefore we have to be very careful with the thoughts we send out into the Universal Information Exchange.

Just as with any telephone connection this is a two-way line. Our individual input is crucially important to the state of the Field!

Every morning wake up and count your blessings.

Say 'thank you' loudly (all sounds are registered in the Field), wish good health to anybody you can think of. It doesn't matter whether the day is sunny or whether you have a stressful meeting scheduled, we must create a positive image of the day.

The Great Cosmic Plan delighted me with a chance to be in Hawaii to join a small group. These people had fought for a long time to gain access to their sacred sites. Now they were determined to reactivate a very special place right on the cliffs over the ocean.

This was where the ceremony of regeneration was to take place. Several days ahead of our group a number of Hawaiians, Maori and Americans had made camp overlooking the ocean.

As a New Zealander I was particularly interested in the similarities between the Hawaiian and Maori cultures. Not that I could know more than a tiny portion of their culture.

I was stunned therefore, as we approached the sacred site, because an elderly Maori man came up and greeted me with the traditional pressing of noses, saying, 'Ah! I know who you are!' And he didn't mean my family name!

No more words were needed. I was a navigator. A traveller comfortable in any realm.

This man carried the tribal knowledge of Maori and provided a bridge between the two largest Polynesian groups.

The welcoming sound of conch shells broke the silence which had fallen over us as we all acknowledged the land, our ancestors and the deep feeling of being 'at home'.

Then as we turned to form a circle someone glanced out to sea. Far, far out in the distance a sight one could never believe, greeted us.

From all directions pods of dolphins were coming to the foot of the cliffs where we stood.

Breathtaking.

They leapt and played and chased each other for perhaps 15 minutes, then just disappeared back to the ocean as mysteriously as they had arrived.

How did they know that this event was happening? Why did they come at that very moment? Not one minute before or later.

Shall we call that a 'miracle' or must we accept it as just natural?

Flight 105: Flight Plan, Cockpit Check and debriefing

SPINS

1. Have your logbook at your side. A favourite pen at the ready?
2. Check that you are relaxed, comfortable. Mental seat belt clicked.
3. Headphones on the ears to hear the music of the spheres, or the commands from the higher self.
4. This flight is for advanced students.
5. Leave your pen on the table. Pick up your closed logbook holding it in both hands. Holding it reverently. It represents your past, present and future life.
6. Are you happy with who you are right now? Ponder that.
7. After a long pause, *slowly* open the book to the photo of yourself you have pasted inside. Look on yourself. This is the most beautiful being that God has

ever conceived. How lucky to be born in this exact century.

8. By now we are on a journey together into some strange territories of the mind. Have no care we are not about to go into an unintentional spin down from the heights. A spin is like a stall with a flourish! When you try too hard to correct the stall, the sudden lack of air under your wings makes the nose drop frighteningly towards the spinning landscape. There is only one thing to do. Apply opposite controls and hang on. And wait. Slowly the spin corrects itself. Harmony returns by the law of nature.

9. Write down the times when you have felt your world is in an uncontrolled spin. What was the outcome? After all the fear, did you crash?

....

10. Can you imagine how to prevent this distress?

....

11. Are you flying too high, or just gliding along with the engine turned off?

....

12. How would you explain what you have experienced to another person?

....

13. To a friend?

....

14. To a stranger?

....

15. To someone with real problems?

....

Place your logbook in your lap, close your eyes and listen outwardly to all the sounds around grounding your thoughts.

16. The Matai

It was time to say goodbye. Standing in the parched tropical sun with the blinding flare from the crushed white coral runway, we hugged not in desolation but in the deep conviction that we had run the mile and completed the tasks we had set ourselves.

Even so it wasn't going to be easy. I would leave and she would stay.

Her father, Matai, nodded to me across her shoulder. There was no recrimination, no judgement. How could there be? He knew of our love and the many times of our tears and confusions.

We knew it was time to let go.

He had supported our journey through the long relationship, but his wisdom shone over all and made the parting one of memories to treasure. A joyful expectation of new beginnings.

As Hemingway might have put it, 'not in sorrow but in freedom'.

Yes, it was just such a classical setting. The things a romance story might have spawned.

Beyond the reef the white surf of the vast Pacific ruthlessly eating away at this speck of coral island, cheekily challenging the might and storms of the great endless need to remove all obstacles in it's path.

At our feet, the impossible blue of the Aitutaki lagoon.

Around us as we kissed the last kiss - yes - the palm trees *did* rustle. The quiet moment of our hug was joined by the eerie whistle of a coconut committing hara-kiri - falling to it's own destiny. A death of form but the birth of life.

There was the theatre of expectation provided by the pilot's nonchalance as he leaned against his tiny plane, quietly waiting until a completion. It was a parting he must have witnessed a thousand times.

And the echo of Vaiotu's aunt whispering her prophetic benediction – *'You will never return to the islands'.*

We had met far from those verdant isles. In Sydney.

Vaiotu's husband was dying of liver cancer, and she, a trained nurse, was devastated that she could do nothing to alleviate his pain, let alone expect any positive help from conventional medicine.

From his love for her and his final wish that she should not suffer more, he wrote her a long letter and walked off into the heat of the Australian bush.

During the three weeks before he was found, she had asked the counsellors of the Cancer Support Group if someone might help her in her grief.

What she needed was a shoulder. A fresh tissue. A listener without ready answers.

After a few visits – perhaps spread over a month - I broached a question that kept arising which I needed an answer for. During each conversation it had intruded like an unfinished picture hung on the wall of her apartment. The frame was clearly in focus, but the subject within it, unclear. A painting waiting for the artist to bring a flash of inspiration.

What was it that causing me, each time I arrived at her apartment building, to get the *feeling*, no, I was *hearing*, the keening of mourning women?

Then, looking out from the tenth floor balcony across the waters of Sydney harbour I would feel a creeping feeling at the back of the neck.

Something odd. I asked Vaiotu why I had never noticed any men around. None in the car park, none in the lift. Her friends were all women. Silence. Long silence.

She told me that the man downstairs had been bedridden ever since he and his wife moved into this block of flats. The husband of one of her friends upstairs had died recently. Most of the other places were rented by single, separated or separating women.

The silence became even more intense. Vaiotu – fearfully? – told me that exactly one week after her husband's body was found she came home one evening and a parrot had somehow squeezed through the very narrow window gap and died in the middle of the lounge room carpet. That parrot was a male.

The same fate came to a budgerigar another friend had given her.

If nothing happens at random, then we should be able to unravel this mystery.

But we needed help. I turned back to the knowledge I had gained from two Koori elders (do not use the word 'Aboriginal' which is a Latin word and is quite abusive if you think about it).

They had helped me to see into the landscape and, with a little investigation, I found the answer to this perplexing phenomenon.

Before the arrival of foreigners, this area, a rocky inlet of the harbour, was where women would go to mourn the loss of their men. Not a burial ground but a special place for ceremony. It was a hair-shivering revelation.

What to do? The first thing to do, if you are sensitive to the natural surroundings and the ancient wisdom of the Koori people, would be to leave the area without disturbance. Of course, no logically minded person is going to vacate an apparently perfectly normal building on the say-so of a 'witch doctor'.

But you can make your own choice as I suggested Vaiotu might do.

Which she did.

Together we did some rituals, which may have had echoes of her own culture helping the spirits become calm and reside in lovingness.

At this time I was closing my clinic and she decided to leave her apartment. Was it so strange that it dawned on us that we both had the genes of the traveller; both islanders... born always setting out for the island on the horizon?

It was a natural progression from friendship to loving the journey, to the closeness of love.

It was travelling to northern parts of Australia, on to Hongkong, Thailand, Malaysia, Burma, Nepal, the Philippines. Everywhere blessed by wonderful people and mind-expanding experiences.

It was a joy of living. It was sometimes hard work ... and neither of us were exactly young chickens!

One day, I clearly remember sitting under the shadow of a giant pagoda in Pagan when she told me her story. At the time of her birth people lived in houses made from the leaves of palm trees. The rafters held many insects and surprises! At the moment of her birth, her mother screamed as a scorpion landed right at the baby's feet and then vanished. Her uncle shushed the young mother, saying 'don't you know what that means? The girl's name must be 'Vaiotu'.' (How he deduced that, has been lost in the mists of mysticism).

In the language of the Cook Islands it translates as: 'vai' - to speak in public; 'otu' means to redress slights which have caused divisions in the family.

We had embarked on the greatest journey you can ever undertake. Opening your backpack to the winds of uncertainty.

There were so many travellers' tales but if you want them in a book, you will have to ask me to write it! Here are two stories in brief. We were travelling in a four-bunk overnight train from Rangoon to Mandalay.

One of our companions was a man from Washington. He spent the entire night inconsolably grieving his friend who had died of AIDS. He was trying to forget and we comforted him.

The other was an elderly woman carrying two guns on the way to Thailand to take revenge on the person who had killed her son in a dope trade which had gone wrong. Sometimes keeping your mouth shut is the best answer!

In the Philippine Islands we were held overnight as hostages by a rebel group. And so on.

If you were travelling in a space ship on the

way to the stars, you could look down on the planet and see the entire Pacific Ocean. Using your amazing digital telescope you could zoom in on the centre point and find the Cook Islands scattered around just south of the equator.

Zoom further in onto the most beautiful atoll of all, Aitutaki, and you would be viewing such exquisite beauty that your immediate impulse would be to abort your mission and return to earth because it can be compared with nothing else in the Universe.

Imagine white sands. Think palm trees waving in the slight breeze and a lagoon such a bright blue that even Mr. Kodak himself would flinch.

Vaiotu's homeland.

We decided it would be best if she went ahead to spend time with her family before I came. And so, several weeks later we met in Rarotonga and together flew the one hour to Aitutaki.

At first Matai and I had some very strained conversations, then slowly he came to accept that I was not just a dancing flower.

He began teaching me simply by doing things.

For example, sitting cross-legged on the cramped trampoline of his small catamaran, he taught me how to catch fish. First you feed them, then thank them with a prayer then give them time to decide who should be caught that day. Most important was to take only two of them. The first one caught must be eaten raw and what is left must be returned to the lagoon. The second would be taken home for the day's lunch.

Only catching what we could eat at one meal.

His legitimacy as a *matai* – the holder of the spiritual knowledge – could not be questioned.

Three mornings a week and Sunday, before the tropical heat set in, the whole village would dress in their best clothes and go to the church established by the British Bible Society and after a desultory hymn or two, the congregation would begin vigorously chanting.

One particularly entrancing chant drew my attention. I asked Matai (the matai takes his role as his forename), 'that was very special, was that chant from the ancestors?'

He looked at me as though the sun had fried my brains. 'I wrote that one,' he muttered, forgiving my ignorance. Then, seeing my surprise he added, 'I am an ancestor'.

Walking away from the church along a palm-fringed avenue he stopped. He was a tall man with the build of an athlete; his black hair turning silver, his deep brown face showing the features of a lifetime living in the tropics.

He was not squinting in the bright sunshine but holding my attention with the lift of his eyebrows and slight upward tilt of the head.

He could have been saying, 'Did you get it?'

There are no ancestors, no descendants. No Time separates us from Space. No yesterday nor tomorrow. All the rest is the illusion created by the

western mind.

A gentle breeze, or that seagull flying by are all coexisting with us, right here and now.

I thought how different and how refreshing his view was to the fashions of modern psychotherapy.

This was in direct contrast to the ideas of isolating and dissecting an individual life in a futile desire to reach harmony and beauty. An approach which I had seen so often result in no more than a larger folio of unresolved questions.

Matai jogged my mind to remind me of that odd word in Polynesian, Whakapapa (*fokker-popper*). There are several interpretations but the most under-stood one is the apparent repetition of patterns we inherit from our ancestors...but we don't have any!

Instead we all live in a goldfish bowl of interconnectedness which gives us the opportunity, whilst in the physical state, to make changes not possible in the spirit world. To correct their mistakes or misunderstandings.

Yes, anyone who cares can easily see that each of us have patterns which both give us pause for distress and those which bring delight and comfort.

We might call them Family Patterns because we seem to have a lot of them closely knitted into the fabric of our relationships. Perhaps an uncle and a grandfather both committed suicide. Aunts or mothers who stay in an abusive environment. Some of us feel that everything we do fails, as it did for our parents and their parents. On the other hand a successful actor may come from a line of artistic people.

It is not a reflection of their genes but their passport to existence.

The question is, even if we can see that this path leads to comfort and delight by acknowledging this information, how may we transform that into joy?

Whakapapa tells us that the purpose of our lives is not embedded in long struggles of investigation but a bright, schoolchild's acceptance of the lessons which have been given to us at birth. Sitting up and paying attention is all the 'teacher' requires for an A grade pass!

It is as simple as that. Once you accept this, you can take a summer break!

Just put a flower in your hair and breathe in the freedom of release from stifling suppression.

Patiently Matai had explained that not just people but nature is endlessly interwoven with us.

Vaiotu had willingly given me the space to spend time with Matai.

Now we must move on. Me, to return to travel. Her, to marry and have children.

17. We Don't Know

We simply have to accept that we don't know.

Perhaps we will never know.

It was a cold day in January when I met Karin at the Centraal Station in Amsterdam.

She had come to show me to the place I was to give a two-day seminar.

Despite the crowded tram we were lucky to get two seats.

It takes about half an hour to get to Overtoomstraat and Karin asked me to fill in the time by telling her what I was going to lecture about, as she would not be able to be there.

And so I told her how I had originated the practice of teaching Intention In Action which grew along the way into Deep Field Relaxation.

Focused on our conversation, we had not taken

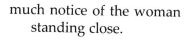

much notice of the woman standing close.

When we did turn to her, we saw that she was crying, the tears streaming down her cheeks.

At that moment the tram stopped, the doors opened and she hesitated before stepping out.

Looking at me through her tears, she reached out as if to touch my shoulder and said, 'Thank you, thank you so very much. You have given me the answers I have been searching for, for a very long time'. The doors shut and we continued on our way.

We don't know *how* it happens.

This is the joy of Not Knowing.

The Nobel nuclear physicist, Richard Feynman told us of not knowing, 'All scientific knowledge is uncertain. This experience with doubt and uncertainty is important. I believe it is of very great value and one that extends beyond the sciences. Some scientific statements are most unsure, some of them are nearly sure, but *none* of them is absolutely certain. We know that it is enough to be able to live and not know'.[4]

That is all very well as a theory. How to *live* with that insecure feeling is not so easy.

It is not important to know *how* it works, it just does.

It is scientists and science who want to know *how* it works. They promise us that they will give us all the necessary answers, often through all those lovely television science programmes.

The answers they provide do not make our lives easier or more full of meaning.

What we need to do is to find how to become comfortable with uncertainty. This is frightening for people who have grown up with ideas of Newtonian science. Thanks to this 'science', for the last two hundred years we have grown to see ourselves separate from nature, each other and the events around us.

In the last two hundred years science has changed our lives (and the planet) forever. We can now, for instance, travel and live in places where we are not at all compatible with the climate we were born into. We can eat bananas in Akureyri in northern Iceland under the Arctic sky; New Zealand apples in Tokyo and Norwegian salmon in South Africa. We use so much oil that we go and kill other people for it. And in case we get lonely, instead of walking to the dance hall, we can sit at home reading all about the world's tragedies on the Internet.

In mediaeval times people worked 14 hours a week. We are not so smart when you think about it. Today most of us work more hours *each day* than their

SERIOUS NOW, JOE!
IF WE CHANGE OUR QUANTUM STATE
ONCE MORE, THAT GUY'S REALLY
GONNA MISS HIS WEEKEND!

entire week's labour.

There are good things to be said about science, but right now I cannot think of too many.

Trying to disguise the fear created by 'scientific truth' many of us spend our lives *dreaming* that our ship will come in one day and when it does, we will be excruciatingly wealthy. From that moment everything will be sweet. We will own the island!

Well anyway, you can thank me later because I did a test run on it for you. In the interests of research, I went out of my way to find a genuine desert island out in the Pacific Ocean – no people, no running water, no television, no mobile phone tower! In a word, deserted.

I asked Matai's brother to take me across the lagoon and, to his obvious amusement ('who would want to do that?'), leave me marooned there for three days on the pristine white sands where no other footprint had ever been.

Just as I suspected, there were no tensions out there. But there are no such islands any more in the world.

The problem with that approach is it cripples our potentials. The one thing worse than going to sleep while we are alive is the false promise of optimism.

Optimism is anaesthetic for the lazy mind. It gives us the excuse to avoid the struggles of the real world. The truth is, if we are constantly waiting optimistically for the cavalry to arrive, we are likely to run out of ammunition before they get here.

No one can know what will happen tomorrow. Tsunami, hurricane or earthquake. And the only moment we know is *now*.

Most of us at some time have been faced with making a serious decision.

Change our job. Try for a new relationship. Which ice cream flavour to choose!

Like children in a toyshop we cannot know which one would give the highest pleasure.

It is the uncertainty of the choice which makes us nervous and tense, often leading to depression. Faced with an unknown outcome we smartly push away the confrontation and lapse into the state of being comfortably numb! Pretending that we can make the decision another day, thereby avoiding the terrible mistake of picking the wrong box and ending up with the booby prize. Our friends, adding to our insecurity, obligingly provide as many variations to the answer as we have friends.

You might think of it as a downward spiral – it exactly feels like it.

We could say, then, that **most depression arises from indecision.**

If we go back to the chorus of our theme song, 'we don't know', and we hear it clearly then the only way out is to give in and join the choir.

Once there was a man who was a constant traveller in the days when most travel was on foot. This meant he had to carry in his heavy knapsack enough food for a day or so and sufficient clothing to survive the weather. In Australia he would be called a swagman (he is carrying his entire belongings on his back in his swag). Perhaps in another culture, he was called a hobo, a gypsy, a nomad or a carpetbagger. In any case he knew he had to find a job soon but had no idea where.

He wasn't being hampered by struggling up and down mountains, nor suffering frostbite or baking in the Sahara sunshine. Just a nice, flat path.

Then he came to a fork in the road. Should he

take the left fork or pick the right? He has heard that the left way might lead to a great job picking fruit...all you can eat! The other road looks equally inviting. Even at this distance he can smell the scent of a rose garden.

But it is too difficult to decide.

He turns back in the direction he came from and tells himself, 'I am doing the right thing. After all, if I go back at least I know what *is* there.'

He is about to step off when a horse and carriage race past, heading down the left hand road.

'Maybe', he thinks, with sweat forming on his brow, 'maybe that was a signal to take the left path.'

With a heave he gets his roll onto his shoulders and turns to head off down that road, happy at last that he did not have to take responsibility for his choice.

Then he falls into a terrible state. God, nature or Jungian synchronicity - one or the other - did not agree with his argument. Because as his head turned his ears heard the sound of a bird singing from the direction of the right-hand path.

Desperately unsure, he just started walking down that one.

He walked and walked. And walked again. His mind was in torment.

'Perhaps,' he reasoned, 'I must have had a mental breakdown because I am sure I should have taken the left road'. 'No, no', his logical brain interjected, 'the right one is the best.'

What was concerning him most was that the path began to take a definite curve. Not the way he wanted to go at all.

At least, he reassured himself, wherever it took him, it was better than sitting back at the dusty junction getting depressed.

As the evening approached, to his great surprise and joy this right-hand road looped back and joined the left one exactly at an inn where he earned a large meal and a bed for the night by curry-combing and hosing the horses.

We could turn our traveller into an avatar - a man of wisdom - if he could just learn how to make *any* decision within his moral and ethical beliefs and then let go of the outcome.

This is what I call (in big letters), The Return To Joy.

18. Deep Field Relaxation

For a long time I was looking for a name for my practice. It came to me suddenly. After I had stopped thinking of it. It was one of my young patients who very quietly said after a treatment with me: 'I think I know now how it is to be connected to the Field. I just dived deep inside it, like into the ocean and then became still. And the wave carried me to where it was necessary. The deeper I went, the more powerful it became. I wasn't afraid of the depth - the water was soft and strong at the same time, it washed away my worries'. I thanked her and since that time I have called it Deep Field Relaxation.

Later on when I travelled to Asia and started learning Qigong (an ancient form of Chinese healing exercise) I heard a very interesting phrase – 'go with the flow'. That phrase reminded me of the story of my patient diving into the ocean.

'*Going with the flow*' is a direct expression of the fundamental principle of Taoism, where we are invited to respond to the flow of Universal energy, to the ever-changing Field. And if we slide on that wave we can easily achieve the state of *wu wei* – 'action without action', 'non-doing'. I usually tell my students at the beginning of each seminar – we will learn how to do nothing. Many of them become hesitant and ask: 'how can you charge somebody for teaching nothing?'

There is nothing in *wu wei* about laziness, drowsiness, inertia, disinterest or mere passivity. Quite the opposite - we are fully involved and yet there is no 'work', no usual attempt to control results. We can relax completely once we are cruising on that wave - the claws of our ego loosens and the Universe has its way.

Do you know that the same principle of not interfering completely changed the practice of agriculture in Japan and some African countries? They just plant the seeds in non-treated, non-ploughed soil and Nature takes over. Their results? Great crops, no use for chemical fertilisers, not much physical effort and a restored ecobalance.

DFR is neither a therapeutic method, nor is it a concept. It is a way of living life. Because the main motto of DFR is 'serving others', it suits professionals of all kinds - teachers and doctors, flight attendants, natural therapists and social workers, managers and customer consultants - anybody who deals with people.

The rules of living life in Deep Field Relaxation are simple.

Rule number one: In all our humility we need to admit that no one can know precisely the cause, nor the remedy for somebody else's problem. The ever-changing world never allows us to know exactly what another person needs at any given moment. The cause of their illness or psychological distress may be a virus, or maybe an inherited disruptive life pattern. Or the wrong type of diet or negative thinking. If you believe in the idea of a past life, then a trauma arisen long ago may be the cause.

Rule number two: Always remember: your state is contagious. It's like this. If someone yawns, people all around begin yawning whether they are sleepy or not; a professional comedian focuses on one person in the audience knowing that others will follow. If 'I' bring myself to a state of quietness, if my intention is to serve the purpose of harmony and balance, then 'you' will be positively affected without further effort. There is actually no 'I' or 'you' – we are all **ONE**.

Rule number three: Your actions are spontaneous, natural and effortless. Someone is crying? Just sit with them. If someone is overwhelmed with fear after a bad medical diagnosis, just remain calm and be sure that the Field will provide support and guidance.

Rule number four: Nothing is impossible for Nature – if some 'miracle' has ever happened, even once, it must be one of Her Laws.

Rule number five: There is no need to be attached to the results of our actions, we don't think of personal profit – fame, acknowledgement or gratitude. We may never know the real results. Very often people are secretive or not observant, too, often they have very high expectations and don't notice the subtle changes.

As long as our intentions are pure and we choose ethical means, '...things will come right at the end if you take care of the means and leave the rest to Him'. (Gandhi). Referring to capitalistic values, Mark Twain said that 'God does the healing but the doctor sends the bill'.

Rule number six: Feelings, sensations and intuition are very important in practicing DFR. They are like a compass navigating the ship in the vast ocean. We don't resist any experiences or feelings as they arise. We allow them to come, we sit with them and then watch them disappear. We know deep inside that our actions are not ego-based. They happen in that particular moment of need, without thought of profit.

We have to be very clear about our intentions of participation in this 'no-work'.

Why do we do this? Is it really what we want to do? What is our goal? And the list continues.

Intention is the control column of the plane. Without it the aircraft has no direction. The intent to serve, to heal, may result in healing even in the absence of special energetic activity.

This suggests that consciousness can develop changes unmediated by transfer of energy. And this is the main difference between DFR and other known approaches.

Rule number seven: Nobody channels energy to anybody. We don't follow any set protocol or written formulas, we don't do any manipulations. There is a complete openness in the way IT happens.

Heaven knows what Nature Herself would think of the title DFR? Does it really matter? What matters, is, that it brings to you the joy of experiencing the Field, its omnipotence and omnipresence.

One friend told me that until he tried DFR, he never really knew what it felt like to be relaxed. The nearest he could get to it was to imagine a quiet, secluded beach. Then he learned how to let go of the conditioning of the mind. Do that, and you can even hear the sound - Tsummm! It occurs when the mind and body is calm and settled, feeling safe. Daily concerns fade, moods soften and new possibilities became clear. The Life Force is able to act without interference from the constant babble of the chattering mind. Doubts dissolve and new horizons in our physical, mental and spiritual bodies open up.

Let's have a look at a brief script of a DFR session.

A patient, Rebecca, arrives at the clinic:

REBECCA: (Enters very quietly, hesitates as

she sits on the edge of the padded leather chair) Mr.Sanderson, I know, because everyone told me that you are the very best healer in the whole world...

ME: (Feigning humility) Well, actually...

R: I've brought all my x-rays to show you, this was me in 1974, you can see the lung, there on the right...and the kidneys in this one, this was taken in 1985, no, no, just a minute, it was '86...

ME: (Politely interrupting) Ah, that won't be...

R: ...I know it was 86 because that was the year my dog bit the ear off my daughter...

ME: (Checking the time) I do hope she has recover...

R: ...it was soon after my doctor told me I had terminal toenail congestion. No one has ever been able...

ME: Let's see what we can...

R: ...Oh, I am so sure that in one session you can miraculously solve all my troubles...could we possibly also include the difficulties I am having with my new neighbours...

ME: I can understand that....perhaps...

R: (Reaches into her portable filing cabinet for a folio of copies of her doctor's prescriptions ranging back for the last 25 years. She points a long, accusing finger at the top one.) ...now this one didn't do

anything for me. At first I thought I felt
something...are you understanding me...

ME: (I take the cue and stand up, move
towards the relaxation couch....Nods.)

Fortunately with DFR we don't need to go into
all the gory details – those cases we file under the
heading of 'DFR – Don't Forget Rebecca'.

The correct script looks more like this:

Rosanna arrives in plenty of time to rest after
her travel, spends a little time with a warm drink.

ME: (Inviting her into the work room). Hello
Rosanna, please come in.

ROSANNA: (Smiles) Shall I lie here?

ME: (Nods. Smiles) Actually we do not do
much talking. In DFR we honestly recognise that it is
impossible for anyone to know exactly what is needed
– the causes are too deep to be revealed by our nearby
mind.

RO: (She's not so sure) I...see.

ME: (I make her comfortable, a blanket is
handy in case she wants it, a cushion snuggles under
her head) Now, let's see what we can do. (The
emphasis is on the *'we'*.) Please make yourself
comfortable on the reclining chair while I switch on
the *Mind Music* CD. Feel free to move at any time. Try
to keep any questions until later.

To an observer nothing happens for twenty minutes. I just seem to sit there with her head cradled in my hands. She just seems to lie there, breathing slowly, eyes closed.

There is something marvellously reassuring, calming, *safe*, when we have someone simply hold our head without any manipulations, no requirement to speak, no demand to 'record' the emotions or physical sensations. It creates a beautiful, intimate silence.

After twenty minutes I quietly leave her to rest for another twenty minutes, much the same as a good acupuncturist allows time to absorb the energy before welcoming the person back into this old world.

What has happened? Oh dear! The old question! The answer is, no one knows for sure! This golden link between the intention, the mind/body reaction and the greater cosmos has eluded science for centuries.

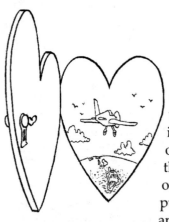

The best guess is that if the 'therapist' (that's nearly as bad a word as the 'healer') has achieved a state of *wu wei* – no worrying thoughts, no fixed ideas of what is happening or what has to be done for this person, then the wisdom of that other person's body pushes through. Both yours and their energy levels harmonise, reach the same mark. If *my* mind is settled, then we, the two people involved, join together in a Field of magic possibilities.

And still the mind continues to worry – 'what IF as a health practitioner (teacher, doctor, social worker, etc.) I might not be doing enough? Isn't it too easy to assume we can make a difference in a serious situation?' My answer to that – *we are honestly doing the best that we can.*

Whether we are trained practitioners or just beginners, we have to admit that some of our answers are most unsure, some of them are nearly sure, but *none* of them is absolutely certain.

Clever, logical people demand to see the data of how many people are actually helped from my work. The short answer is that even by changing their attitude or beliefs enough to visit a 'healer', they have begun to change. I then go on to say that every single person - that is 100% of the people who come to see me, dies. The only variable is when!

Understanding of Deep Field Relaxation comes not from learning a complex theory, but from forming personal experience. Many people who were diagnosed with a month or two to live have called me 15 or 20 years later to say, that not one week has gone by without remembering what they had experienced during a DFR treatment.

How marvellous! How incredible! How outrageous!

But, do not get carried away with the excitement. The truth is, no matter how much you start bouncing on your chair desperately wanting to tell *anyone* the Good News, mostly they find other things to be occupied with.

New ideas have always been ignored. We are not alone in that frustration. The history of science is full of examples where new ideas were crushed.

Naval surgeon John Lind in 1747 discovered how to prevent scurvy. The lack of vitamin C was the British navy's number one killer. The Admiralty took 49 years to do anything about it.

Dr. Ignatius Semmelweiss, in 1848, urged/pleaded with doctors to wash their hands in chlorine after working in the morgue before delivering babies in the maternity wards. More than a million women died unnecessarily because the doctors were incensed that they were being held responsible for the transmission of disease. Semmelwiess was mercilessly persecuted by his colleagues.

Even today the ideas of German physician Samuel Hahnemann on homeopathy have been scrutinised and ridiculed by the medical establishment. That, despite those remedies have no damaging side effects, that homeopathy is a multi-million-dollar business and that nearly every health insurer in Europe now (partly) compensates the use of homeopathic medicine.

But wait, by thinking about unfortunate scientists, we've nearly forgotten our logbook!

Let's make an entry soon.

>> Number One: Your role is just to be calm within yourself. Not expecting, not rejecting. Go with the flow, IT knows where to go.

Number Two: If you want to be of service to others, do not think of yourself as a helper, because if you do, you will be creating someone who is helpless. You will feel superior to those who are in need. It is enough to make it clear that you are ready to spend some time with them. Simply say 'Let's see what *we* can do.' We are both being served in such a case, we share the space. *Together* we try something which is not intrusive, neither does it demand standing on one leg for an hour each day.

Number Three: Each of us is specially gifted and there is no one who is more spiritually advanced than any other person. We are all intimately connected.

Having an ego is necessary, parading it around is not.

How many of us have taken our medical histories to one therapist after another. We sit there reciting the accepted diagnosis knowing deep inside ourselves that there will be no magic pill, no sudden alleviation of symptoms. But what if the 'therapist' says, 'Dear Anna (or Ferdinand), I have no idea what your problem is, let's forget the recitation and just spend twenty minutes of quiet time.' How shocking is that? *How dramatic!*

Finally, honesty! The patient's mind doesn't know which way to turn. Why are the African witchdoctors, the balian of Indonesia, the Egyptian priests and the jankris of Nepal and others trusted by their fellow villagers in all possible and impossible situations? Because they don't pretend, and together with the patient they pray and dance asking for the answers from the Gods.

So? What is left for us?

Slowly we start to throw away the complexities and arguments which arise with things we cannot know for certain. Then comes the knowing that you know for certain that you will never know, and the glorious thing is, it ceases to matter any more.

The Role of the Healer

The role of the 'Healer' is to guide the
mind into that moment of silence
when miracles are possible

Immediate results, though often oc-
curring, are not sought, for it may
take years, perhaps generations for
today's changes to mature

Therefore the 'Healer' patiently
abides in the silent knowledge of
allowing, for allowing speaks of
proper relationship with the eternal;
of creative participation in
the plan which lies out beyond the
span of a single lifetime

Thus comforted, the mind, within a
moment of quiet understanding, experiences
a vibrant knowing of
the Spiritual Universe

19. The Film

Twenty years before the film *'What The Bleep Do We Know'* was made, I had written an original script along the same lines. This was in 1976 and by 1982 we were on location in several countries shooting under the title *'God Doesn't Play Dice'* - a play on Einstein's comment. I wanted to discover the connections between the statements of well-respected scientists and psychics.

Tataucho Muhuawit gave a little smile at the frustration I was showing each time the interview was interrupted by my cameraman's coughing.

The young medicine man of the Owl Tribe lay back in the Californian sunshine casually waiting for the next take. Finally he signalled to me to wait a moment while he cast his eyes over the surrounding trees. Then he walked over and selected one leaf which he brought back and handed to the cameraman.

'Chew on that,' he offered.

From then on the shot was completed without any noises on the sound track.

This was interesting to me and while my crew packed the equipment, I asked him what was that leaf?

LISTEN, PALS, THE ONE WHO DRAWS A BLANK TELLS HIM THAT WE FORGOT TO PUT THE NEW ROLL IN...

'It's not just any leaf,' he smiled, 'it has to be the right leaf for the right person at the right time. In the Field of Existence,' he went on, 'these plants, those trees, the moon are all one.'

Several years later, in southern Brazil, Evalina Navarette, who grew up 'three months travelling from the nearest post office', demonstrated to me the same use of the practical relationship with nature. As her jungle disappeared under the smoke and chain saws of the insane, she gathered together as many incredibly rare therapeutic plants as she could, and moved to the tiny town of *Iguazo* where she opened her house and garden as a Pensione. She spoke her local language as well as Portuguese, English, French and German.

In quiet evenings as the sun mellowed and the dust of the day settled, she would instruct anyone interested in the lore she had been taught by the elders of the tribe. One time as we sat listening, one of her cats began attacking a nearby bush.

'Ah,' she said, 'malaria.'

'Pardon?'

'Malaria. If you show any signs of malaria you must chew on the topmost leaves of that 2-metre shrub. No malaria.'

'Ahem. You say that eating those leaves relieves malaria?' I suspected the answer she might give but I went ahead and said it anyway. 'Why don't we package some leaves and become millionaires?'

She graciously smiled at my impertinence, 'because, they only work if you live near that particular bush. In the next village it might be a completely different plant to get the same effect.'

Meanwhile, back at the scene of the filmmaking, Tataucho's words were clearly proven by the fact that over the next 12 weeks there was not one cough or sneeze.

After Tataucho I talked with Dr. Jim Hurtak, ex-NASA scientist, author of 'The Keys of Enoch' and other books, the man who first described the pyramids and face on Mars. He had read my research, and was so cooperative that, had I been filming on videotape instead of 35 mm film, we could have made a documentary right there and then. What he left me with was the stunning concept that we are all co-creators not just of our own lives but of the Universe itself.

It echoed well with my understanding of the belief held by the Koori people of Australia. They are certain that if they do not re-create the world each morning, it would cease to exist – more than 120,000 years later quantum physics tells us much the same thing.

Are you getting the feeling, as I did, that unconsciously I was creating my own path?

Sometimes that path was difficult to follow. Thomas Banyacya – the true holder of the Hopi prophecies, was an impossible man to contact and seldom gave interviews. However, I called his home in *Kyhotsmovi* and surprisingly his wife said he would be happy to be in the film, if he wasn't out in the desert at the time. It sounded like a polite way of saying no. I couldn't risk my budget on an uncertain chance, so I took his name out of the list and didn't schedule him into the programme.

A month later a funny thing happened when I was teaching a meditation class in Sydney.

>> We were practicing the way of 'meditating outward', that is, instead of 'emptying the mind' which most of us find completely impossible, we sit and listen to the natural sounds around us. It gives us a feeling of interconnectedness with everything within the Field and unity within the group.

Without any intention to do this, and for the

first time, as I relaxed, I found myself speaking out loud with exactly the voice of an American Indian. Can you imagine how much resistance I had to doing this?

In psychic circles and in spiritual groups there 'always' seems to be an Indian 'guide' who channels words of wisdom. So when Banyacya with his gravely voice spoke through me - who else could it be – said 'we will meet soon'. That was it. I knew the film would be made.

Apart from his uninvited visit to the meditation group we had no more contact until six months later, when I arrived in Tucson with the film crew to interview a professor from the university. Without much hope of catching Banyacya, I took a chance and called.

His wife immediately answered, 'yes I have just driven three hours to put him on a plane. He knew you were coming,' pause, 'only thing is, he doesn't know which hotel you are staying in!'

When he arrived I took him to dinner. Walking from the hotel to the restaurant, our first chance to be alone, I asked him, 'was it really you who came through me assuring me the film would happen?'

We might have expected him to turn on his heel and head quickly back to the desert. Instead he kept walking and began a quiet chant…. 'hum a he yah, hum a he yah, hum a he yah'. Like that.

When the student is least expecting it, the teacher gets you by the scruff of the neck and kicks your bum …hard!

We went on to do a great interview with the glorious backdrop of the Painted Desert. He generously gave me lots of information not usually shared – especially not to a wild bunch of Australian filmmakers!

Or perhaps that is why he did! I was so happy after the shooting that I completely lost my left brain and asked him if he minded if I took one or two still photos of him, realising even as I said it that it was an inappropriate request. His hesitation told me that I had crossed the line but he allowed me to take three photos.

Don't be surprised - when I had the film processed those three frames were completely black.

On another occasion I was following up my research on the world's changing weather patterns and I found myself in the Negev desert interviewing Bedouin Sheik Hamad. At first he correctly pointed out that only Allah knows the future, and we shouldn't try to outguess Him. But as we sat around the coffee jar he began telling poems which the anthropologist/translator had never before managed to extract.

Listening and looking out at the barren sandy landscape, I marvelled at how his people could possibly have survived for so many centuries in such arid conditions.

I gathered he said something like, 'We must not make prophecy, but we *can* predict what might happen based on past events.'

With a shrug of his multicoloured robe he waved his hand to follow as he shuffled out of the black tent into the hot sun. From inside his clothes he took a small bag of salt (as treasured as gold in the desert) and he made six little piles separated by equally small stones.

It seems that there are only six months of the year when it might rain in the desert, and so husbanding the scarce grass is a survival skill. Each October the predictor would place his piles of salt on a flat rock, leaving them overnight. In the morning the dew would have formed little rivulets of water on some piles, another might be just a little moist, others dry. His people had perfected long-range weather forecasting by accessing the Field of Information.

Now it was time to dig out a scientist and confront him with these possibilities.

Biologist Lyall Watson, author of *'Supernature'* and other best sellers, immediately picked up on the theme of God not playing dice. He cut directly to the heart of my project, or perhaps I should say, eye.

As we stood in Richmond Park, London, he pointed to the herds of deer nearby.

'Darwin knew that there was a major flaw in his 'Theory of Evolution', Watson told me, 'when he considered the vertebrate eye, it sent shivers down his spine'.

A fully operational eye could not have evolved. Either the eye worked or it didn't. Without it, the animal would not have survived. The eye must have sprung from the evolutionary pool as a fully functional item. If it did not, then you wouldn't be reading this, even with your glasses on.

Recently I read in Bill Bryson's *'A Short History of Nearly Everything'* that fossil records before the Cambrian age show no evidence of any vision at all. In fact very little life of any sort. Then, suddenly trilobites with complex nervous systems, limbs, gills and a 'brain of sorts' appeared with the strangest eyes ever seen.

As if these creatures had mysteriously arrived by galactic express.

Watson had said, 'we are confronted with what appears to be a planned, effectively instantaneous, evolutionary leap. As a scientist,' he went on, 'I find it hard to accept, but if we can see there is a plan, then clearly there has to be a planner! A 'God' if you like.'

What does all this tell us?

The first thing is to get some humility in the face of knowing so little about the place we live. How little we remember about being in harmony with nature.

All this yes, but, what a wonderful, joyful, creative, supportive, organised place the Universe is!!!

Without any help *life just is*!!!

Flight 106: Flight Plan, Cockpit Check and debriefing

AEROBATICS

1. Have your logbook at your side. A favourite pen at the ready?
2. Check that you are relaxed, comfortable. Mental seat belt clicked.
3. Headphones on the ears to hear the music of the spheres, or the commands from the higher self.
4. Without any hesitation pick up the pen and write down the date and the exact time.
5. By now we should be getting comfortable with Not Knowing. Review and describe your progress on that.

   ....

6. This flight we are going to need an instructor with us - your intention - to grow through confronting confusions. It is the time to let go of limiting fears. We are going to dive and climb

and scoot all over the sky.
Laughing, watching the ground
loop around to become the
clouds as old ideas of security
dissolve like late-winter mist.
Join in the joyful spirit of letting
go. Think what you have never
been brave enough to just go and
do. Dancing until 4 am; running
bare foot in the frosty grass;
meditating nonstop for three
hours; discovering the
confusions of your educated
mind fighting with your
intuitions.

7. If you could do just what you
    want to do right now, what
    would you do?

    ....

8. Spend a day with people who
    are ill. The path to pleasure is
    through service to others. Make
    a list....

    ....

Aerobatics is what most of us do for much of
our life. Distorting our bodies, minds and emotions to
please others. To agree to be scared of *being* different,
agreeing to accept the politically generated fear of
neighbours, those who *look* different, those who don't
wish to be subservient to the mindless 80 million
sheep!

20. The Tibetan Lama

Not by chance (have I said that before?) I found myself in Lhasa, Tibet. You can be sure I had always wanted to go there, but how to do that, was the question.

It so happened that my friends and the monk I spoke of before were travelling from Hongkong and I was invited to be in the group.

What I didn't know, was that Professor Geoffrey Hopkins, one of the Dalai Lama's translators was also there to celebrate the Buddha's birthday – the first time in 50 years the local people had been permitted to do this. How lucky was that? He could speak perfect Tibetan and knew exactly how to act within the culture.

It so happened that his partner had some stomach problem and although at first Geoffrey was sceptical about my work, he changed completely when the problem disappeared after two sessions with me.

There were also a group of European monks and monkesses (!) sorry, nuns, who were curious about healing.

We had some wonderful debates whether my work fitted into the Buddhist Way (it does).

Knowing Geoffrey literally opened doors for me. The most amazing was the visit to the personal quarters of the Dalai Lama in the Potala palace.

One moment, uno momento! It is time to point out that the whole reason for telling these stories is to underline that:

1: You do not need to become a wandering vagabond to gather into yourself all this fun and freedom.

2: You do not need to leave your partner, family, the dog, canaries or whatever, because you are already prepared. Just keep reading mine or any other material that floats past. Absolutely any situation can be seen as a chance to learn.

3: You may have to give up watching the television news. Sorry.

What happened next definitely changed my life in ways that could not be estimated before or later. I believe it could do the same for yours too.

Through Geoffrey I heard that Gen Thabka La, the Abbot of the Sera monastery had had a stroke.

He had tried the Chinese doctors, Tibetan and the Western hospital with no success.

He was unable to lift his arms, which was extremely serious because, an old man now approaching his death, he had been preparing himself for many years for his transition. The physical actions he wished to perform included certain arm movements he considered essential.

To my astonishment and humility he agreed to my visiting him. Can you imagine me not only in the presence of such a person, but being welcomed into his inner sanctuary?

Geoffrey was soon leaving Tibet and so he wrote out translations of any sentence I might need and this we used for the first four sessions. Then a French student appeared and that difficulty was resolved.

The only question left for me was, how to touch his head as part of my treatment, since it is extremely rude to touch another person's head in most Asian cultures. In this case I had little choice and he submitted readily. What a joy it was. He was like a child at Christmas, if you don't mind the mixed traditions.

He would welcome me with a great smile, always something to offer in the form of a *thanka* (cloth icon) to see, or a statue which probably came from Noah's Ark – or earlier.

We smiled and nodded heads and waited for some sign of change. It came on the sixth session.

That day I was met at the door by the French student. He told me that Gen Thabka La did not require me and I was about to turn away when he spotted me around the brocade curtains and motioned me in.

With gentle hands he showed me that he could lift them above his head. If I remember rightly there is no such word as 'thank you' in Tibetan, it is assumed that you have been thanked.

What he did was so moving that I had a little tear in my eye. I think he did too.

He took me by the back of the head and pressed our foreheads together. The highest form of blessing.

Through the translator I understood him to say, 'We don't know.'

He had been the Abbot of the biggest teaching monastery in Tibet. Most of his life had been instructing, debating and living the Buddhist way.

Yet I got the impression that for both of us, our meeting had brought about a dawning of deepest clarity.

I cannot say just what he had felt, but, from then on, I found myself completely comfortable saying, 'I don't know.'

21. The Joy of Saying Yes

If this is true, then the only way to navigate your life towards happiness, good health and greater purpose, is by relaxing, allowing Nature herself to guide your footsteps.

If we can never be certain of the outcome of any decision how can we possibly navigate to our joyful centre?

If we cannot find a path to the right answer, doesn't that leave us in a very big mud pool?

Well, yes the answer is......yes.

Fortunately there are ways to circumnavigate the whirlpool!

And we must start from the wrong side. To know 'yes', we first need to know 'no' and a few 'maybes' as well. Then there is the sneaky one. The

'Yes, but...' which disguises itself as a 'yes', but is really saying 'I disagree with you, I am not even listening to what you are saying. I am just 'politely' waiting for a chance to butt in and correct your mistaken ideas!'

Let's start with the obvious no's. We will have no argument that there are some positive 'no's'.

In fact it is a good idea right now to make a list of the ones which come to mind without delay.

Here are few which I can think of:

- no to drugs of any sort
- no to abuse of alcohol
- no to physical abuse of any sort
- no to sexual aggression
- no to smoking

There are more – keep a page in your logbook to add any that you can think of.

These are the ones which are as clear as two + two = four, for all people - whether living on the planet Earth or trespassing in the far galaxies.

Then there are the no's which apply in some cultures and not in others. The 'maybes' might include - in Malaysia, for example, it is perfectly legal to have up to four wives. In others it is highly illegal.

On the other hand, when I was in the highlands of Nepal, I talked with a young woman who told me that she had two husbands – one was a Sherpa helping mountaineers, the other a businessman in the city. The only argument was over how much time she would spend with either.

I have read that in some communities in the Pacific it was expected that a young woman had to have had a child before she would be considered as a marriage partner.

To the Maori, the correct greeting is to lightly touch noses. Try that in England and it might be a fist, not a nose, you might be greeted with!

So there are a great many things which have developed as traditions in different parts of the world for different reasons. They are not intrinsically damaging, just designed to make society tolerable. Of course they consist of an unending list of do's and don'ts an adult person is required to observe. They are dressed up as statements of personal right.

Then there are the ones which are not so precise. The ones most people more or less agree to. The sort of controls which have grown into the fabric of individual groups. We call them cultural morals to assure ourselves that they are to be respected and obeyed. They are also the ones which are used to control the unthinking populace. The sleeping ones. The seriously comatose.

Many of these artificially applied rules are total nonsense to any mentally sane person.

Think about these ones for outrageous conditions of life in my village. It was considered, amongst her peer group, a scandal if my mother did not have the family washing done and hanging on the line before 10 am. Even worse was if she dared to do it any day except Monday – the agreed day for washing clothes!

At the height of the Cold War, if we enjoyed a slice of lemon in our black tea, known as Russian Tea, we were at risk of being accused of having communistic leanings. And so on.

Here is the point.

Apart from those big no-no's, saying 'no' crushes creativity, fun, enjoyment, personal satisfaction and, not least of all, brings the death of conversation - the 'Yes, but….' blocking tactic.

But to say 'yes' is to open all sorts of

possibilities.

If we want to find our own Tulip, we have to give ourselves space in our cramped minds to allow for new things. Unknown things. Unproven things. Things which, after the event, we can look back and see that nothing tragic hit the ice box!

Instead of depression and confusion, life becomes a blessing! All those imagined sufferings dissolve away; they fly out the window like Peter Pan on a night sortie.

You think it is easy? Of course it isn't easy. Ask any fledgling what it is like to leap off the edge of the nest on their first solo attempt. Then, within weeks, they cash in their mileage tokens and take off from Freiburg or Friesland heading for Freetown or Fremantle.

The conversation goes like this:

Momma Bird: 'I've done feeding you all the worms you can eat. It's time to look after yourself. Take off!'

Frightened chirper peering fearfully over the edge of the nest: 'Why did you have to build this thing so high above the ground? I could kill myself stepping into space like that.'

Poppa Bird: 'Do you want the neighbours to think I brought forth a quivering disgrace to the Swallow community? Jump now, or I shall pluck your tail feathers with an eagle's claw!'

He jumps.

Moments later the miracle happens. Within an hour he is zipping all over the sky shouting, 'Come on you old fogies, let's get going, I always wanted to see Bangkok at night!'

Bangkok may not be the preferred destination for all of us. Perhaps we are looking for a better job, a wider group of friends, improvement in relationships or freedom from money worries.

It all starts with the BIG YES.

In little ways and great big ways we see these things all of the time. The trick is to learn how to live with them daily. And encourage them to be your shadow.

As they say, there are many ways to peel a peach; none are exclusively right, none fail totally.

One way to encourage the yes technology is to consider it as a form of intuition. For some reason 50% of us, the Yins, are supposed to have a natural ability called 'women's intuition' and the other 50%, the Yangs, the male populace, are known for their impenetrable brains!

But what is the rule? What works for one must be possible for all.

So, taking our courage in one hand we must begin to listen to our feelings. What feels good to me? What do I secretly dream of? What are the bounds I have set up for myself and why? How can I know that letting go of all those restrictions will get me into a better place than I am right now?

Richard Bach[5] gives us the clue:'Just be who you are, calm and clear and bright. Automatically, as we shine who we are, asking ourselves every minute is this what I really want to do, doing it only when we answer yes, automatically that turns away those who have nothing to learn from who we are and attracts those who do, and from whom we have to learn, as well.'

If we grow to be comfortable with all of that, then we can face up to the fact that every 'yes' carries an equally confusing 'no'. We can never go outside of our convictions (the Big No's) but far too often we leave ourselves in a sort of miasma of blank intentions watching the sunset over a barren landscape.

It is time to go back to the stories.

And I have some cracking good ones! A little later we'll talk about how I got to be eating radiated food from the Chernobyl meltdown. But first we go back to Sydney Australia, where I had a clinic seeing patients with all sorts of problems including people from St George's Oncological hospital.

It was very successful but after three years, for *no apparent reason* I decided it was time to move on. With no purpose in mind I put a few things in the car, tied my bicycle on the back and headed north for the warmth and easy way of life in tropical Queensland. That was the first yes.

Not by chance, great friends of mine, Jean-Claude and Arriane were in Townsville. At that time I could never have known that 20 years later Jean-

Claude would write the best selling book, *'Going Deeper'*.

When they left to go on to Hongkong, I went north to Port Douglas to spend some time following my passion of daily riding uncounted kilometres. Sleeping in a tent at a basic camping ground, trying to avoid the mosquitoes, snakes and crocodiles.

You get the picture. Tropical fruit, no cares in the world, humid days to lie around reading or writing and riding the bike late into the cool of the night. A man should be so lucky!

Then after just a few evenings the night manager caught me as I arrived back from a great ride, and called out, 'Are you Clif Sanderson?'

'Yes,' I said, surprised because there were only two people in the world who knew where I was - Jean-Claude and Arriane and they were in Hongkong.

'You have to call Hongkong urgently,' I was told.

What could they want?

Jean-Claude came on the line, 'seems the Universe doesn't want you to have a holiday,' he said, amusement in his voice. Then he became serious, 'remember that business card you gave me when I mentioned we were going to Hongkong?'

I certainly did. I had only met this lady once two years ago at a Healer's Congress in the Philippine Islands. I have no idea why I kept her card. Let alone why I was carrying it in my pocket.

'Well I called her. Her mother is seriously ill and asks you to come.'

'Now?'

'Now.'

Standing there in my riding shorts, dripping wet after the humid ride, my bicycle leaning against my leg, the sound of the cicadas almost drowning out my words, what could I say?

It took me less than an inbreath to say, 'YES'.

Did I ever mention to you that I am a dedicated traveller? I am one of those people who, as a child, would sit and 'read' a map for hours on end. Tasting the delicious thoughts and anticipations of new challenges, new experiences and new people with new ideas. At the same time unable to envision myself following the gypsy caravans.

Two days later the ticket arrived. Three days later I arrived in Hongkong still dressed in shorts and sandals.

It was more than a dream come true. Not only was I able to use my ability to help a suffering person, but in an 'incredible' way it gave me the key to much of my further work.

Are we clear here? The 'yes' did not come from out of the blue sky. I was not suddenly expected to become an architect or an accountant, it was simply an extension of the path I was already following. My intention had long been to be of service to others, and here was evidence that the Universe reciprocates the good we do.

The fact that I was totally happy about the developments, is probably why my presence affected Miriam in a surprisingly powerful way. Within days she was back at work in the busy manufacturing world she ran with her husband.

I cannot tell you her ongoing medical history because soon after working with her I was invited by one of my new friends to work the magic in Norway. But I understood she survived considerably longer than was expected.

From this sort of story you can tell I am a dedicated promoter of 'YES' therapy.

It never lets you down.

The thing is: Do not believe in it. Do not *trust* it. Come to *know it.*

Remember. Remember. If it works for anyone, it works for you.

... IT'S A TRAVELLER!

22. The Moscow Surgeon

In Stavanger, Norway, Brigit, a schoolteacher, had been too ill to leave her home for nearly a year. After several sessions with DFR, within a week she was out looking for a job. I know that she survived more than a year beyond the expected time. This success was significant enough for me to be invited back for a series of visits each summer over three years, to see people and work in clinics and with private consultations.

It was during one of my visits there that an American friend, Tanya, whom I hadn't heard from for four years, called me from Pittsburgh, inviting me to visit Moscow where she and her husband would be teaching English for a year.

The famous 'yes' flooded my senses and poured out of my mouth as quick as a flash. This time it was even easier to say because I immediately saw that I could stop over in Moscow en route to Sydney for my son's wedding. Ah! The synchronicity!

All she said when she met me at Sheremetyevo

airport was, 'Welcome to the Paris of the Nineties!'

I hardly had time to put my suitcases under the bed before she told me I should unpack my good shirt as the Russian Ministry of Health was holding a conference on integrated medicine. They had heard I was coming and I was billed for a two-hour speech the next day.

All went well with the presentation I thought. I was enjoying it, listening to the Russian translation and ready to answer questions.

Instead of a question, a short elderly man stood up and in a voice creamed with authority, loudly proclaimed, 'I have never heard of this, I find it hard to believe.' There was a rustle in the audience, swords were being drawn, and a plague of sceptical sniggering broke out.

I thought, 'Oh well, back to the holiday.'

'However,' my interlocutor continued, 'if you would come to my hospital, I would like to check it out.'

Unknown to me, Professor Evgeny Stranadko was the leading cancer surgeon for the former Soviet Union. He was head of the Russian Oncological Hospital in Moscow.

Early the following Wednesday I was led into an auditorium full of doctors and nurses.

After a pleasant introduction I was asked to begin demonstrating in a way which I consider highly dangerous.

Throughout the day, patients were brought in one by one and I would be asked to give a spot diagnosis of their condition; the doctors being aware of the medical history and condition of the illness.

We got off to a great start when the first man brought in, was in a wheelchair. I scanned his body and proclaimed that there was *something missing* from around the lower part of the stomach. This might have been thought a little vague, but I have deliberately not learnt the intricacies of physiology and keep my assumptions more or less general.

A hush came over the audience accompanied by a growing buzz. They knew that this man had just come from an operation to have a portion of his ulcerated bowel removed.

Stranadko stayed with me all day, asking

questions, checking with his colleagues the accuracy of my work and, towards the end of the afternoon presenting to me a woman who I declined to work with.

'You must tell us about this woman's condition,' he insisted.

Again I resisted. 'I would prefer not to' I said.

'We want you to describe this person's state of health, *pazyalista* (please).'

What I had seen, was that she was in perfect health, and after a hesitation I told them so.

'That is correct,' the professor smiled. Apparently I had passed the test. He told me: 'I am impressed but not yet convinced, can you come back tomorrow?'

What I had been practicing is not so difficult to do. Either through a natural ability or with a little training almost anyone who chooses, can do what is termed *medical intuition*. It is very fashionable.

This is the recognition of the state of another person's body by scanning their Field and 'feeling' the condition. It requires an open mind coupled with a lack of logical interference.

However, the danger lies in the mind of the patient. What if I misdiagnose? What if I am accepted as a great medical intuitive, then what? My authority impresses the mind of the patient and if I tell them that I see, say, a problem with their kidneys, their anxious mind begins to brood over it and confirms the prophecy with a physical outcome.

This would be a clear example of unskilful action. Therefore, I only do this when demonstrating in a doctor's presence and with the patient's agreement. In this case I have to operate on two levels.

On one, I would read the *doctor's* mind and be impressive with my accuracy, confirming the agreed diagnosis. On the other, the ethical side of it, was that if I could see a different picture of the illness I simply allowed appropriate change to occur.

By the time I arrived the second morning the word had gone out on the telephone network and more than two hundred people were waiting outside the hospital. Unfortunately we were unable to find the place or time to see them until much later.

The research began with an event which conclusively convinced the sceptics. The man who had had his intestine partly removed *walked* into the auditorium. That was impressive. He told us, 'I drove myself here, but I need the same energy as yesterday to get home again.'

With such support, on that second day, I was able to introduce my own views and by the end of the day Stranadko understood that this method could be taught. He was sure it would be helpful for his patients. He said to me, 'Now I am convinced, you must teach me and all my doctors.'

And now a little amusement. How was it that it worked so clearly for me when the minds of all of the doctors and all of the patients were thinking not in English but in Russian? Fascinating! When we get to talk about the Field of Creativity it helps to know that the universal knowledge is available anywhere at any time without so much as a CD-ROM to help.

One thing I did learn quickly was how to say *'pectopah'* in Russian. Everywhere I was practicing reading the word pectopah on signs and hotel lounge rooms. Imagine my delight when I discovered that, by an odd coincidence, the Cyrillic letters in pectopah are the same shapes as in Latin. However, the 'p' reads as 'r'; the 'c' the same as 's' and the word is pronounced restauran (t). Important information.

What a time it was! A group from the conference decided to meet in the forest of Sokolniki Park on Sunday to discuss what we might do together to increase the recognition of integrated medicine. There were three Russian doctors, two nurses, an American doctor and his wife, a nurse.

At the end of the meeting, as we stood up we noticed two women nearby, one of whom was in obvious distress. It was soon seen that she was experiencing heart failure as understood by the doctors. However they did not have their machinery with them and were unable to help other than measure the progress of the problem. With a nod from one of them, I stood behind her and placed my hands on her shoulders. By then she had stopped breathing and her heart was not pumping. But, within a moment she gave a loud gasp, her heart started and by the time we began to walk towards the road she was sitting up on the park bench happily chatting with her friend.

Does this happen spontaneously to many people? I do not know. It was enough that the story was mentioned in the newspapers and led to television appearances and invitations to work with almost all of the medical colleges and clinics in Moscow.

On one occasion I was leading a meditation group in a clinic and my driver, a young Russian friend of Tanya's, was present. Often as we drove between appointments we would have long discussions. He showed himself as an entrenched disbeliever.

As the evening came to an end he stood behind one woman and waved his arms in all directions at once, making a joke that he was a great healer, while we made smiling faces at each other.

Next morning as we arrived at the clinic the same woman came running up to Kostya, grabbing hold of his sleeve. In high excitement she demanded he give her another healing session.

A little nonplussed he pulled back but she insisted, 'after that session in the hospital last night the scar on my face disappeared!!!' Sure enough it was confirmed that what had been an obvious scar, was no longer there.

We cannot leave it at that. It confronts us with a discussion on whether 'miracles' are possible.

And so for a short while we have to leave Moscow, coming back to it soon.

23. What's possible and what's not

What is a 'miracle'?

It comes down to this: *can* it happen or *did* it happen?

If we say, 'It is possible', then the correct answer is 'anything can happen', because our minds are the most incredibly creative computers imaginable - Bill Gates, eat your heart out! Perhaps there is life on Mars! Maybe the little green men from the Pleiades may, one day, step off their craft for a goodwill visit!

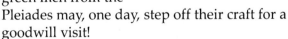

It *can* happen – we cannot deny something we

cannot disprove. But *has* it happened?

In the case of the woman who lost her scar, all her friends could *see* the change. What is not possible is to know *how* it worked.

And this is where we depart from the world of Western science.

The law of science demands that an event must be able to be recreated over and over.

However, it is obviously impossible to find and bring together a room full of people each with scars and then expect that, with a wave of the wand, the scars all vanish!

There are far too many factors involved.

Edgar Cayce was the world's most well known psychic. Many books have been written about his amazing ability to diagnose whilst in trance. He was regularly featured on a radio program called, 'Ripley's Believe it or Not' where visible and experiential results of his work were revealed.

I recall one of his successes. Cayce had given the parents of a dying child a prescription which he insisted must be filled by a particular pharmacist in a particular apothecary in Ohio. The frustrated pharmacist could not find two of the ingredients. When the parents returned to Cayce, he went into his usual trance and exactly described how they could find the missing ingredients. He said they would find them on a high shelf in that drug store. Now, they went back and looking harder, saw that many years before when the shop had been remodelled, the top shelf had been covered. With the agreement of the shop owner they pried it off. Amongst the ancient bottles and the dust of nearly a century were what they were looking for, and that child's life was saved.

It did happen.

Let's turn back to the theme song of our book, the chorus line runs like this: if something has been observed to happen even once, anywhere, anytime to any person or at any place, it can happen again.

The caution is this. Did it really happen or was it imagined? Was there actual evidence or just hearsay? We have to be very careful before we spread the good news!

Sometimes life is so unbelievably sweet. I always remembered hearing that story and so you can imagine how happy I was, when I had the opportunity to interview Dr. Jim Windsor, who in 1983 was the director of the Edgar Cayce Institute in Virginia Beach (USA). He was a gentle, helpful man.

In the foyer of the Institute stood a very large black and white hand-coloured photograph of Edgar Cayce. I wanted to film that and had my crew set up the powerful lights we needed. As we watched, Dr. Windsor told me of a very interesting event which had happened the previous week.

A tourist from Texas had taken a snapshot of the same photograph. When his film was processed, it showed Cayce had his eyes closed.

Jim had sent the film off to Kodak to check if it was genuine.

You might imagine what a wave of psychic eruptions that would have engulfed the world if it was proved.

He stood beside me as I asked my assistant to turn on the lights. They came on and there, before our astonished eyes, we saw Cayce close his eyes.

If we switched on the lights, the eyes closed. Switch off the light, the eyes open.

On close inspection we found that the photopaper had been polished by the colourist working hard to get the right tones in the eyes, and on certain angles under the bright lights of the movie camera the lights reflected back to the viewer. Creating the illusion that the eyes closed.

What a smorgasbord of questions arose! Had I

not been there at that exact time with my lights, there would have been a very important error spread. Many people would have assumed that Cayce had sent a message from the 'other side'. How was it that no one in all the 30 or forty years had ever captured the same effect as that Texan?

If there *was* a message from Cayce in it, I could only imagine that he was telling us that we need to be *very* careful when we assume to know anything at all!

We have to be very very careful if we choose to make any psychic statements. We should really try to avoid promoting that sort of thing!

On that same day, again it could not have been just by chance that Gladys Rice Davies was on one of her rare visits to the centre. Now an elderly lady, she had been Cayce's stenographer all those years and had long ago stopped giving interviews. But she was happy to confirm for me that he would never have liked to be called "The Sleeping Prophet" which some authors insist on naming him.

All this doesn't deny the incredible borders of our imagination.

Can we truly declare that reincarnation is what

we will all go through when we leave 'here'; are there really angels, spirit guides, God, sunny Mondays and life after Elvis?

'Maybe' is the nearest we can get to it. No matter how desperate we wish it, all those questions remain for the pleasure of the awake and the confusion of the fearful. There is no supportive, concrete evidence.

Somewhere between these two poles, the fantasy world of the mind, and the logically valuing mind, lies the third state. That of experience.

Those who knew the woman with the scar know without doubt that it is no longer there. To them, what happened can no longer be considered impossible. They have seen that such a thing happened. For them, denial is not possible.

If so, then we must agree that such a 'miracle' can probably be reproduced, despite scepticism and the restrictions of science's level of understanding.

If, for example, dozens of children suffering explosive nosebleeds as a side effect of living in a radioactive zone, find relief through the actions of a 'healer', it is highly probable that the method can be adopted as a way of alleviating this suffering.

What does this tell us? Simple. When the controlling mind gets out of the way, no matter *how* it happens, miracles *have to* occur. There is no point in reading this book and then throwing it in the back of the bookshelf. What a waste of your time if all you can do, is hit your head with questions and doubts. Get out of the way and just Do it! Do it!

24 More Than Probable

We now need to spend some time looking into the usefulness of knowing ' we know nothing.'

By starting from that understanding we can build a useful, practical platform to work outwards into a life free of the beliefs of others. In this chapter I want to share with you the stories of just a very few of the happenings. They can give us a basis for acknowledging the power of focusing on the probable, rather than the fantasy of what has been 'sold' as true, when in reality it *may* be possible but needs to be taken with care.

As the people of this most blessed generation, we are the first who can travel wherever we choose, to be able to indulge in any culture we fancy, to make judgements not available ever before.

Unfortunately for the last two to three hundred years science has successfully convinced us that the way to know the make-up of the Universe, is to pick it apart like a chicken pecking at grits. As if the human mind could eventually create itself, if only we could just find the right formula.

The trouble with that is far too much happens way outside of the scientist's mind - a sort of blindfold which is tightened by his accompanying sceptical narrow beliefs.

Fortunately there are people who, acknowledging that they can never know precisely what they are doing, have a good chance of being right. Their works show remarkably miraculous probabilities!

Read on for more fun and fascination............

In November 1984 in the mountain city of Baguio, Philippines, Jun Labo sponsored an international healer's conference.

A few of us were privileged to be present as he gave his daily consultations for nearly 300 people at his *Munsayac Inn* healing centre. Of all the well-known practitioners, Jun was the most renowned of the psychic surgeons. The rumour has it that he had cured one of the Japanese Emperor's daughters, who promptly married him!

All the same I was careful to reserve my belief until I could actually watch him work.

Early in the morning a large number of people would gather in his chapel for religious singing and a sermon of sorts to the anxiously waiting patients. Some had been to see him before, others were sitting nervously glancing side-to-side wondering if their long journey from countries all over the world, would magically remove their illnesses, or would they be exposed to a very clever charlatan. Who could tell?

Despite their fears the singing became more and more energetic as the congregation joined in, watching for a sight of Jun; but he kept out of the way.

I wondered, as I would many times, if this was really designed to keep his presence as mysterious, as unapproachable as possible. He must have known that an important part of shaking up a person's mind was to act in an exotic, incomprehensible fashion.

For example, the true African witchdoctors must have well understood the power of being odd, strange, even threatening to their patients. They must have grown up in their small villages amongst their peer group but once selected to be trained, to be effective, they were required to learn a special language, to wear feather head dresses, unique

clothing and body decoration. The shamans of
Siberia, the balians of Indonesia, the tohungas of Ao
Tea Roa all created an atmosphere of fear if not at least
unapproachability.

Here in the mountains of the fabled Philippine
Islands it was no less awesome for the patients to be
subjecting themselves to this ritual healing. There was
unquestionably a tangible atmosphere of reluctance to
move towards the operating room.

The room was quite disappointing. Just a large
empty waiting room with a very small room at one end
with a large viewing window, allowing observers to
clearly see the operations. Inside there was barely
space for a flat table, the operating table. There was
nothing else in the room except a small metal rubbish
bin (to collect the body parts?).

Casually two helpers were spreading a white
cloth over the narrow table. Still holding my sceptical
mind in check, I checked that it was possible to see
under the table. There was nothing hidden there.

As the time came, the patients slowly formed
into a long snake bending around the waiting room
facing the operating theatre. You need to understand
that most of these people had come from European
and American countries.

Many were having extreme difficulty following
the instruction to strip to the waist in front of all of
these strangers. One rather overweight English lady
tried hard to keep facing the wall, only slowly
overcoming her embarrassment. Others put on a brave
face while hugging their breasts or attempting to
nonchalantly stare out of the window.

This, I thought, was a very clever move on the part of Labo. The more the person's mind is diverted by an unusual, even awkward space, the more the impact of change comes about.

Then, with a flourish, he strode into his tiny working room. There was a perceptible gasp, a change in the atmosphere in the room. At least now there was something to focus on other than the bare bodies. From this moment tension began to rise as the dreaded movement of surgery approached. All eyes were on this slight, intense man. No more than 1,5 metres tall, with his deep black hair carefully combed back off his shoulders, immaculate finger nails, his unexpectedly muscular arms reaching out of his short sleeved open-necked white shirt with brightly embroidered front panels.

As with many Filipinos, he wore his shirt outside his trousers... a political statement lasting from the days of Spanish dominance of their country, when the ordinary people were forced to wear their shirts inside their trousers, to discriminate them from the ruler's forms of dress.

With a friendly smile he waved to the three of us who had been invited to observe. We moved closer to be just outside the window.

Then with a bigger smile, he held up his open hands in the traditional magician's signal to show that he could not possibly have anything up his sleeve. Ever the showman!

From holding his hands above his head he lowered them directly onto the stomach of the first patient. Immediately a squirt of red liquid (blood?)

splashed against the window opposite my face.

I know enough about stage makeup that theatrical blood capsules are effective when, say, the actor is 'punched' in the mouth...the fake blood can only dribble out – not in a one-metre stream.

Labo went into his speciality which was what he called his 'psychic x-ray'. As each patient was invited into the operating room, they were asked to pause standing in front of him while he held a white sheet at arms length, 'reading the illness'.

Slowly the bucket filled with bloody rags, used cotton wool wads and what appeared to be body tissue.

Next patient. Before John went into the surgery, I asked if he would mind telling me his problem.

'I've had a cyst under my chin for several months, the doctors cannot help me'.

Sure enough, after his quick x-ray, he lay down and quick as a flash Labo took his fingernail and slashed across John's neck. A huge amount of pus flowed into the kidney dish held by one of Jun's helpers.

I glanced at Father Bulatao, head of Psychology for Manila University, who was standing next to me. We signalled 'uh huh' to each other by raised eyebrows. If this man was faking, he was certainly a master magician!

I thought again, 'Could all healing be simply a

highly active placebo effect?'

Here was convincing evidence that what is probable, will be repeatable. One by one the patients all showed distinctly different outcomes. No research protocol could have possibly determined the percentages of change based on, literally, nonhuman mathematics.

Does it matter?

Next. A Korean man who could not speak English or Filipino (*Tagalog*). He walked away without the limp or pain after his years of suffering.

Yet nothing can compare to personal experience. One of the times I visited the Philippines I was speaking and observing at a healer's conference with 40 local healers in the *Manila Hotel*.

Psychic surgeon Edgar St. Maria caught my eye, 'Why are you keeping that pain in your side?' He demanded.

'Simply because no doctor, healer or

naturopath has ever been able to find the problem or fix it over five years.'

'Lie down', he said – full of confidence. In less than a minute there was the usual flow of 'blood', a great warmth in my stomach, the feeling of energy moving in the area of my pain. From that moment, until today, I have never had pain in that area.

In our conversation he told me jokingly that I was very fortunate with the method I used, because his way cost him a lot of pesos for cotton wool!

Jaime Licauco, a journalist who started out to disprove healing, later became one of the greatest supporters. He gave me another insight. Which I translate here: He found that the impact of the surgery was not as long-lasting as the sort of work I do. Why? Well I suggested that in the few seconds of impact the physical body can change, but the mind does not necessarily have time to agree. It is all over so quickly. The psychic surgeon could bring about immediate measurable changes in the body, but I found that the result of a DFR session, which is primarily an approach to the silence of nature, was considerably more profound. Although it doesn't have the spectacle of magic, it opens emotional and spiritual realms confronting the patient with multiple choices to let go of the symptoms they have often suppressed all their life.

Perhaps the difference between psychic surgery and DFR might be described as similar to the difference between the medical surgeon, who cuts out the tumour, while the true healing happens outside the physical realm. ....the doctor does the surgery but God does the healing.

Still on the trail of what is probable, I turned to the healers of Brazil.

While there have been many books about the Philippine psychic surgeons not so much was known of the healers of Brazil until recently.

Without doubt the most incredible was a simple government worker, known as Arigo, 'the surgeon of the rusty knife'. He claimed that he could go into a trance, then be overshadowed by a long-dead German doctor called Dr. Fritz.

He could take his penknife and thrust it deep into a person's stomach or into their eye and pull it out with no pain, no blood and no scar. Films were made of his work and medical scientists could not fault his successes.

What was significant to me was that, unlike most other healers in Brazil, England, the Philippines and so on, he did not necessarily attribute his work to a spiritual connection, but by allowing his body to be used by this doctor, a discarnate being....that is to say, a human being who could be identified, who had lived before and had learnt medical practices in the 'real' world.

Sadly, Arigo had died in an accident (some would say it was no accident) long before I got to Belem - the city at the mouth of the Amazon River. In investigating his life, I discovered that a number of healers had taken on the name of Dr. Fritz wishing to gain the same notoriety, I was told that each of them had died in accidents exactly the same as Arigo had.

My conclusion: there is no need to make claims

of superior spiritual connections to be a wonderful
healer. Still, over and over, there is a need to learn how
to let go of all those trainings, once you have grasped
them all!!! Paradox upon paradox!

For example, early in my 'career' I had a
teacher who told me that I should never touch a
person's head while healing as the energy would go
down their spine and cause terrible problems. Being an
agreeable student I followed that instruction for a
number of years. Later, I became a friend of a very
experienced healer in London. I watched with concern
when I saw her placing her hand on the patient's head.
I couldn't help myself; I said to her, 'Perhaps you
shouldn't place your hand on the patient's head?'

With some frustration she smiled at me, 'if you
do not do that, it won't work'.

Healing is an art, not a science. You cannot do
double blind research and expect to arrive at
repeatable data. You cannot demand that each healer
should follow the same path. It is sufficient to study
any method, then let it go and let God do the healing.

We have to say over and over again, 'let us see
what we can do' to our patients. The probability based
on a lot of experience is that there will be a significant
change, emotional, physical, or spiritual.

Mind you, when sceptics (don't you love their
arrogance?) or medical researchers demand of me,
'Then, what are the percentages of change in your
patients?', I blandly tease them with, 'Oh, I am sure
that one hundred percent of my patients discover some
change'.

You can see their derision; ready to bring out the knives of their superior complexes.

Of course I do not claim to know exactly what change we might expect for my patients. But the fact that they have chosen to try something, which they cannot know, cannot link to, cannot block, cannot argue with, is enough for me to say that all of their minds have been opened, even if just a tiny crack.

It is enough to know that anecdotes are the stories of life and living and hope, while researchers far too often follow the hearse to the graveyard.

In my novel, 'Earth Bound', I re-tell the old Russian story of a village plagued by something strange destroying the ripened barley crop. They turn to Fedor, whose oldest son had just returned from university. He sat in the field far into the night figuring the equations of possibilities, but long before dawn he fell asleep, tired from his mental gymnastics. The crop was damaged again.

So Fedor asked his second son to help. Nickolai was a practical man. He knew all about inventing machinery. For week after week, instead of harvesting the crop he had the entire village putting all their time and resources into constructing his device. Still the crop was being lost.

With only one son left, in desperation, Fedor turned to his youngest.

Ivanushka Durachock was known as the village fool. He spent most of his life in the forest playing his flute.

One evening of the full moon he took his flute and sat at the edge of the field beside a silver birch tree and played. His music was so entrancing that appeared before him a golden horse prancing with its flowing mane and shiny black hooves dancing on the barley.

No words were spoken, only the soft touch of the music. It was enough for the golden horse to understand Ivanushka's request. The horse bowed deeply and then, with a delightful whinny, flew off across the treetops.

We so easily forget that often it is the village simpleton who, knowing that we can never know, solves the problem. Without effort, a little laughter, a little music lifts the heavy load of being 'normal'. Hah!

Flight 107: Flight Plan, Cockpit Check and debriefing

ENLIGHTENMENT

1. Have your logbook at your side. A favourite pen at the ready?
2. Check that you are relaxed, comfortable. Mental seat belt clicked.
3. Headphones on the ears to hear the music of the spheres, or the commands from the higher self.
4. Open your logbook at your photograph. How are you doing?
5. Review all your entries, what changes, which resistances have you written about and overcome? Are you ready to just let go and accept that 'we don't know' and that that is comfortable for you?
6. Pick up the pen and write the date and exact time.
7. Write down the thoughts that surround you. The ones you are

reading about. The ones that arise spontaneously.

....

8. Pause.
9. Still confused? Desperate for enlightenment? Write it down like this, 'en-lighten-ment'. It means getting rid of excess baggage. Lighten the load of the wild mind. According to my extremely detailed research, we carry around 99.96% more stuff than we ever use. How often, for example will you need Pythagoras' theorem? Does it matter to your kids what the square root of 1120 is? To be light means to laugh in the face of the world.
10. What baggage can you leave behind at the check–in counter of your life?

....

25. Back in the USSR

There is nothing like a practical example to convince others. Especially one which could not have been pre-arranged.

Professor Leonid Makarov[6] tells this story.

'I met Clif Sanderson in 1990, during the first year of *'perestroika'* when a big group of specialists in alternative medicine came to Russia for a conference.

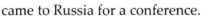

'Clif made the deepest impression on me by the depth and scale of his ideas, through his wisdom and lack of antagonism towards other ideas. This is a quality rarely demonstrated by alternative practitioners in Russia.

'At that time I was in charge of a research

project on the healing effects of subtle energy and I invited Clif to lecture to the staff of the Russian Federation Institute of Paediatrics and Children's Surgery.

'At the beginning of his speech the audience, which consisted mainly of conventional thinking doctors and medical researchers, showed scepticism and distrust.

'But slowly he conquered them with his charisma and knowledge of scientific facts.

'Suddenly in the midst of his speech, to everybody's surprise, one of the nurses who was known to be passionate about anomalous phenomena such as UFOs, healing and telepathy, moved to the stage.

'She started screaming loudly, aggressively demanding that conventional medicine should be forbidden and they must use only energy instead.

'At that moment Clif, who didn't understand a word she was saying, since his interpreter had become speechless, came up to the woman, put his palm on her head and looked into her eyes.

'The nurse stopped screaming, calmed down and slowly left the room.

'Soon after this story we became friends and we worked together on clinical research projects using his technique.

'Very often I saw the healing effect of his presence in the room, even when he didn't touch the patients, but only talked to them. Very often I witnessed people with psychosomatic illnesses being helped where drug based methods had not brought any significant change.

'We know that during certain life situations the defence forces of our body such as immunity, nervous system, endocrine glands become activated.

'From a scientific point of view the mechanism of triggering them is impossible to explain.

'There are many laws of nature which remain unknown to us.

'I see a human being as a complex self-regulating system within the universal forces.

'Our body is designed by God (Nature) in such a way, that it doesn't need to fall ill and if it does, there is a built-in mechanism to get well again.

'It is important to remember that the cause of the illness is always inside us, not outside.

'I can illustrate this statement by the following example.

'While travelling to the Chernobyl zone as a member of medical commissions, very often I found that where there were twins within one family, one of them could accumulate a big dose of radio nuclides and another one – none at all.

'The wholeness of consciousness is the most important factor.

'Clif's method is needed not only for people who are already ill, but as a prevention against chronic diseases of our age, such as cardiovascular disease, cancer and diabetes,' he concluded.

Just how much the mind is responsible for our bad health can never be certain. We are subject to our illusions, delusions and fears. These are exacerbated by the insecurity promoted by all political systems.

In my case I grew up within a culture which thought all Russians were out to take over the world. Films and news reports all created an atmosphere of fear – especially towards their secret police, the KGB.

For this reason it wasn't unexpected that I was more than nervous when confronted by a situation which could easily generate serious concerns.

As Leonid Makarov has pointed out, I was there exactly at the time *'perestroika'* was beginning. No one could be sure whether it had yet become acceptable to talk of integrated medicine, spiritual values or independent expression.

From the news items and my interviews on television discussing subjects, so recently forbidden, it was reasonable to expect some negative reaction from the political sector.

With this in mind my concern rose when Tanya was unable to accompany me to a lecture at a medical gathering. Neither Kostya nor my other trusted driver, Ephim, were available at that time. However the people who had arranged the lecture, organised a car to pick me up.

It was early evening as I came downstairs to be confronted by three large men who could easily have been stand-ins for Schwarznegger. Who else could they be, but KGB agents?

Bravely, but swallowing energetically, I climbed into the confined rear space of the tiny Lada.

No one said anything. None of them spoke English and there was no point in my endlessly repeating 'pectopah'.

In these situations the mind loses time and distance telescopes. I was convinced we were halfway to Siberia already when the narrow, unmade road twisted into a miniature cul-de-sac.

In one corner was a rusting gate to a weed-infested yard. There were no other cars, no lights on in the dilapidated building and no sign of life. I was sure the men had positioned themselves so that I couldn't make a run for it.

A bell was pressed. A light flickered on inside the building. A door slid open and out stepped two huge, huge women dressed in white coats. They took me by the elbows and guided me through the closing door.

It is difficult not to sound dramatic describing my feelings, but let's just say, it wasn't my idea of an evening in Paris.

It got worse. I had noticed it was a four-storey building and the door of the elevator was broken, leaning at a strange angle. But instead of walking up the stairs I was strongly guided towards the basement steps.

Two floors down from ground level the long corridor was lit with barred glass. On either side were, I swear, a row of steel covered doors. It is hard to say whether the white ghosts beside me picked up my nervousness. They just keep inexorably walking me down this line of, well, what else could they be, but cell doors.

We stopped in front of one of the doors. The biggest woman opened the door – me expecting to hear the rattle of the jailer's keys.

Instead the door opened into a brightly lit room. Instead of a gloomy cell, there was a crowd of nearly one hundred people all standing and applauding my arrival. How was I to know this was the auditorium of a psychiatric college!?!

It was one of the defining moments in my history as a healer!

And just how wonderful the Russian people were, and how open-minded and ready to listen and debate in such deep levels of investigation. There were some who were completely convinced of the imminent arrival of space people; there were those who had studied the pyramids of many cultures, others were practiced healers with a variety of modalities. Most were *also* medically qualified doctors, surgeons and a sprinkling of nuclear physicists.

With such an audience, I ventured to discuss my approach to making changes to radioactivity. And, can you believe: there was one man who had brought with him two tiny vials of radioactive material. I held them for a moment or two and he promised to let me know what happened. Some time later I heard that there had been a significant change but the scientist was intent on keeping the results to himself. It was more than 5 years before I had another chance to try again with another nuclear physicist.

In another case there was no question about keeping the results quiet. I had lectured at the Klara Tsetkin Women's Hospital in Moscow. Lecturer Professor Marina Schulova asked me if my method might work for infertility, as her daughter-in-law had been trying to become pregnant for three years.

I was pretty confident, as by then I had seen this approach bring joy to many couples from Hongkong to Norway.

Within two months her daughter-in-law was pregnant and nine months later the celebrations were inspiring when a beautiful girl was born.

At another hospital I lectured to a group of five psychiatrists. After the talk I was asked to demonstrate in the small intensive care ward. There were two women patients, both with postnatal trauma. One was in deep coma. As I began to work with her, from the corner of my eye I saw all the doctors and nurses hastily leaving the room. They gathered outside, looking in through the large glass observation windows. Sadly I found no response from the first patient so I moved to the second who was sitting up with a blank expression.

After perhaps ten minutes she asked for a glass of orange juice. Without knowing the language, I had no idea what she had said, so I called in one of the nurses. This followed a fury of talking among the doctors. It seemed this lady had decided that it was time to die, and for several weeks she had refused to speak or eat, requiring some sort of force-feeding. (From then on she rapidly recovered and was sent home two weeks later).

Naturally, later I asked the group why they had all left the room so quickly. There was, they said, so much energy in the room they could not stay there.

I cannot say that all this time I was particularly aware of the children affected by nuclear radiation from the Chernobyl tragedy. Of course I had seen many of them in the course of visiting the different hospitals.

But soon that was all to change.

26. Chernobyl

At that medical conference in Moscow I was surprised to see an American filmmaker I had last seen five years ago at a soiree in a penthouse in Fifth Avenue, New York.

How I ever remembered his name, I cannot say. And Boris Said certainly did not immediately recall our meeting at the private preview of the film he had made on Credo Mutwa, the last Zulu Witchdoctor.

'Boris Said, I presume,' echoing Stanley's greeting to Dr. Livingston meeting deep in the African jungle.

It took me little time to realise that Boris was the sort of person who could swing an invitation to the Queen's garden party! You could not say he just attracted others to his projects, he fairly engulfed them with his excitement and wide vision, even when – as so often happened – his wildly optimistic projects defaulted before they got fully airborne.

Naturally he was interested in *everything*, which is why he was at that Conference in the first place.

At that time he had several projects 'in the fire' all at once.

And I became his very latest one!

What's more, he was of Egyptian-Russian descent and had a good command of Russian so we had some real fun together. Neither of us had partners at the time and there is no doubt Russian girls are very attractive – even if most of them live in apartments shared by aunts, cousins, uncles and all sorts of relatives.

Before going on to Minsk to do some business, he told me of a very emotional film he had seen about the psychological impacts of the Chernobyl tragedy from the viewpoint of the sufferers.

He insisted that I should be in touch with Ms. Laskova, the Byelorussian film director who made that film.

It was just two days before I was due to leave Russia, but I called her and, like Boris, I was very moved by her story of the real impact on the local people, the effects which media never looked into, and the danger she was in when her filmmaking took her to highly radioactive places.

She also filmed in hospitals where she saw the daily tragedy.

Galina began searching for any alternative solutions.

It is true to say that I was very moved by her story, but I could not see how I could be involved. The feeling, however, stayed with me.

But the hope which had been provoked by hearing of my work in Moscow did not die within her.

Three months later she found me in New York and called to ask, if I would come and work in the haematological hospital with the Chernobyl children.

This directly confronted me with all my theories. Either they worked or they didn't. Within a microsecond I heard myself saying a big 'yes'.

Though once I had hung up, you can be sure I seriously questioned my sanity.

Who, in their right mind, would agree to eat radioactive food; drink the doubtful water; work with more than 60 children (and their mothers) each day? Living with the terrible tragedy of between 12 and 15 children dying each week in that hospital?

I had no idea I would be doing this for the next five years or more.

Before I started work the chief doctor welcomed me with deep resignation. She had seen so many teams of conventional doctors and helpers come from many countries, but there had not been any perceptible change in the death rate of her children. She agreed to my working there with the certainty that this was just another hopeless attempt.

But *fate* stepped in on the very first morning. One of her senior doctors met me at the door with a sad story of her damaged back, 'could I help'. She was bent almost double with the pain. I had her sit down right there and then. Next morning she came running down the hospital corridor to meet me. No pain. Grateful. (So was I, who could know how it would all go in such stressful surroundings?).

I don't think I am capable of giving you the full view of what it was like. Besides it is hard to write as the emotion rises when I think or speak of the sight of one child after another 'disappearing' from the wards day by day.

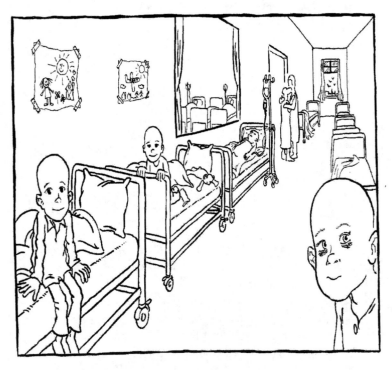

Yet amongst all the horror of mother's crying as their children died; watching as the children slowly lost their battle; as the medicine seemed to add to the struggle; as no medical protocol was found to help – some inner strength seemed to walk the floors.

The kids would laugh and smile when I walked into their ward. They dubbed me the 'Summer Santa' pulling at my large beard and waiting for the sweets they knew would appear by magic from my endless pockets.

Still with no conversational Russian to share, we would make silly faces at each other, tickle the young ones and give a little hug or flick of an ear.

In the midst of these powerful emotions, I had a remarkable insight. What I was privileged to understand was that *some* of these children - aged from one year old to 14 - were showing us that they were completely happy to die. Now that sounds an incredible thing to say. Only by seeing these kids in such large numbers, was it possible to see that there were ones who 'knew' they had only needed to 'kiss the planet' and leave, having completed their cycle of lifetimes.

I am not going to excuse my words. There is no other way to describe what I was sensing. What was even more touching was, that I explained my vision to the parents. And they were able to suffer much less, for they could see and agree with my feelings. We felt that these souls had found a way to come to this difficult world, for a brief time, and through that agreement were able to avoid the whole cycle of human confusion.

Slowly the number of children dying reduced from twelve to fifteen per week to two or three.

Soon the doctors began asking me what sort of prognosis I would offer for each child.

They found that I could predict an approaching illness several days before their technology could diagnose it.

Galina Laskova had worked hard with Boris to find a sponsor who would provide hotel and travel costs and now she was fully involved in translating through all those long hours we stood on our feet moving from ward to ward.

She was the driving force behind forming a group to search for help for the hundreds of thousands of Chernobyl Children. Her own son, Dimitri, 7, was affected too and her fear for his health added to her desire for answers.

The first thought she had had was to investigate Tibetan medicine but she could not find a practitioner who was prepared to come to that area. Homeopathy was considered. Supplements also passed through the sieve but the conclusion, aided and abetted by Boris and my television appearances, swung the vote towards asking me.

We worked and worked and worked. Long hours were spent talking to the mothers. Talking with the nurses. Chatting in the staff room to the doctors.

One day the chief doctor told us that she had had a very severe headache all morning. The staff all insisted that I work on her right away while they watched. Even though her headache disappeared immediately, she loudly declared that the pill she had taken four hours earlier, had started working! Sigh!

Each evening after work Galina would walk with me to the *Planyeta Hotel*, on *Prospekt Masherova*, staying to make sure I didn't fatally annoy the watchdogs – the women whose job it is to sit on each landing making sure no one stole the light fittings.

It was a time to relax, discuss the day's troubles and, as time went by, to begin talking other, less traumatic things.

We had a mutual interest in filmmaking. We talked about her film, not yet fully edited. We shared concern for Dimitri although from looking extremely ill when I arrived, he had changed into a bright, happy boy.

We compared life stories. Mine mostly unremarkable – her with the scars of the struggle inherent in the system she had grown up in. This was true, but she had always been a person with a free soul.

Slowly something new, unexpected, started happening.

The conversations became longer. Holding hands wasn't just to keep warm in the Russian winter. The laughter and the dancing grew.

The law of precession was working again!

In my heart the sun was shining.

27. The Impossible Marriage

When I was leaving Belarus I made an important decision. On the way to the airport I asked Galina if she would become my wife.

And Galina said, 'Yes'.

As the record shows, exactly three months after we met, we married in New York!

How is that for a cosmic 'yes'?

But wait a minute! There's more to come. Once the yes's start coming they never stop!

In New York there was the most incredible hotel manager you could ever hope to meet.

Hans Keller knew of our work with the

Chernobyl children and invited us to stay in his
Lufthansa Penta hotel directly opposite the *Madison
Square Gardens*. In the heart of New York.

Then when he heard we were planning to
marry, he told us that some of the rooms on the
seventh floor were being renovated. He couldn't let
them and if we didn't mind the noise, we were
welcome to stay into the Royal Suite.

Two nights later at 2 am I woke up to see a man
in our bedroom pointing a gun right at my naked
stomach. All the horrors you have heard of about New
York flashed past my eyes. He had come in through
Dimitri's room, which hadn't been locked, so the
intruder must have already seen the kid. The man I
was looking at stood about two metres high, huge and
wearing a ruffled grey suit. Then I noticed another
man who seemed to be hiding behind the door. When
he moved a little I noticed he was wearing a hotel
security uniform.

You know how it is when you are facing a man
with a gun, you sort of lose it! I couldn't remember
Hans Keller's name. We found later that he had
forgotten to tell the night security staff we were in the
otherwise vacant floor and someone had heard us
making a noise there.

The two of us and seven-year-old Dimitri, in
his own adjoining suite, lived free in the exclusive
Royal Suite for the next three months. Can you
imagine that?

In exchange I trained his staff in personal
energy management.

Throughout that time we were able to arrange supplies for the Minsk hospital. Probably few know that the German people and especially Lufthansa were the most helpful during the early years of the tragedy. They would air freight, without any cost, the medical supplies, computers and even clothes for 'our' Chernobyl children.

What a pleasure it was working with them.

When you are in your proper place, you don't need religions or creeds. Anything.

Life does itself.

Here's a lovely one.

Picture London. Staid old London.

As part of a lecture series Galina and I were giving there in support of FOCUS, our Children's Charity, we stayed with Ellen and Bela Hatvany, in their house in Holland Park.

They were generous people who made their house available for the travelling lecturers of the world! Of course you would normally stay a few days then move on.

But, in order to keep doing our work in Europe, we needed to get English residency and a place to stay for some time.

I told my wife we should not go to a Real Estate Agency. Something will come up.

We noticed that we had never seen anyone coming in and out of the next-door garden flat.

Galina asked the owner and she said her house was up for sale but we were welcome to stay there without paying rent until it was sold. As a result we lived in this very exclusive part of London for a whole year!

This unbelievable 'luck' can and will happen for you if you are doing the work you are supposed to be doing.

According to the plan you will always be supported in the most remarkable way.

If you just pause for a minute and think back, I am sure you will remember that once waiting in a long line at the check in at an airport, or buying tickets at a cinema, suddenly you were chosen from among all the others waiting, to be the first person to be served.

28. I am doing the best that I can

'The Tao', said the master, 'belongs neither to knowing nor to not knowing'.

Knowing is false understanding; not knowing is blind ignorance. If you really understand the Tao beyond doubt, it's like the empty sky.' [In a way the Tao is something similar to the Field of Creativity].

There is only one way to answer the paradox of life - do what you can.

Guilt arises when we think we have not tried enough.

Frustration becomes paranoia.

Buddhists have a saying, 'practice skilful action.'

But you can never know exactly the outcome of any decision you make.

The important thing is to make *any* decision.

Trust your inner self. Few people deliberately cause problems for others. Even then, you can turn any experience into a learning time.

I remember Arnold in Sydney. He had been told by his doctors that his cancer was inoperable. You might think that the most skilful action would be to consult every possible alternative practitioner. Instead he decided, 'so what! I've had a good innings, I've always enjoyed my beer, smoking and eating meat-filled pies. Why change?'

He spent his days sitting in the hot Australian sun, getting drunk, smoking and eating large meals. All the things he had been told not to do.

After a few weeks of this he started to notice that the crumbs he dropped would be swooped on by brightly coloured parrots. It occurred to him that they could also share his cancer.

Two years later, healthy and as cheeky as his parrots, he came to our cancer support group to share his inspiring story with others.

He had never heard of creating visualisations. As far as he was concerned, meditating was for the birds and if anyone had told him about spirit guides helping him, he would have taken another swig from his bottle and moved rapidly out of range. In fact he was a perfectly 'normal' person.

Very often the skilful action to do is....nothing.

But that is hard. It takes courage. The natural feeling is to do something. Our ego demands it.

The truth is, no one is perfect. If we were, we would have been saints.

I read that Abraham Lincoln was happy to say that he was correct only 51% of the time. He could accept that and told friends, 'that's why I am the President.'

Do whatever you can. Whatever feels right to do, obviously within moral and ethical boundaries.

Deep freedom comes from trusting our inner knowing that we are doing our best.

the stormy waves
crashing against the
obstinate cliffs are
nature's rage against
obstructions

the fiery thunderbolt,
satisfied,
connects heaven to earth

the mind desires
tranquillity
but stirs the horrors of the
night

when will we ever learn?

29. Breathing

Breathing is what we do.

We begin with a smack on the bum, and we keep doing it until they close the lid.

Breathing is not just about survival. When we want to let go of sorrow, let go of fear, let go of everyday troubles. There is a way. Connecting with the Qi of life – the life force.

We could say that the real meaning of the Chinese word *Qi* is 'life work'…where the energy moves us instead of us trying to make the universe fit into our tiny world.

The passport is already processed and ready for you to pick up, complete with all the visas you will ever need. The open door in front of us invites us to step out into a mythical, magical world.

Anything is possible. Anything can happen. Colours are brighter. The sky is bluer. The horizon is patterned with growth, space and freedom.

>> Take a deep breath. It is all there for all of us.

Breathe in the Qi.

In a quiet moment breathe slowly in, filling the stomach first to full capacity.

Then fill the lungs. Making sure your shoulders do not lift while your chest expands.

Hold that breath whilst counting slowly. 1...2...3...only as long as it is comfortable.

Breathe out normally first out from the stomach, then empty the lungs, holding and counting...1...2...3... and so on.

That's it! Is that simple, or what? There are books and seminars teaching breathing but they only become useful if you keep practicing this form of breathing all the time. At the supermarket check out, when waiting at the red lights, on the train, plane or ship.

Just all day long.

What we are doing is increasing the amount of oxygen in the blood stream. That is what we need more than anything else to increase our health potential.

There are complicated scientific reasons why. Without needing to go into that now, it appears that there is a reaction between the oxygen and the carbon dioxide which drives more oxygen into the blood stream.

For our everyday satisfaction it is enough to notice the changes in the way we walk, think, have greater stamina - and the sun shines more often!

To open ourselves to the highest degree we use this technique to bring peacefulness and a natural slowing down of our speedy minds.

Which brings us to the skill of meditating 'successfully'.

30. Freedom From Meditation

The best meditation is with an empty mind.

Except you can't do it.

Try it!

Despite instructions from the greatest teachers, it is impossible to simply empty the mind. Believe me, I have tried it. The ten-day retreats without talking. The endless nights sitting watching the mind jog around the Universe. The illusions, delusions and never-ending confusions. All I got was a sore backside and a stiff neck!

What, then, to do?

Well, here is the Maharaja's gem of meditation.

Do nothing! Yeah, right! Do nothing. Difficult?

There are several different forms of doing nothings.

One is to drift off into a daydream world.

Not useful.

Then there's the *Contemplating Great Things* fantasy. That's getting closer but the great things you wish for, far too often refuse to turn up in the way you wish.

>> Another is to take the advice of one of my great Chinese teachers, Dr. Xu, who always said, 'do everything effortlessly'. Easier to do, but still not it.
No, you have to give your mind something simple to do! Something which occupies it with nothing. Preferably so that both sides of the brain are co-opted into the exercise. Have I said it often enough to make sure you remember that we are living in a practical world?

The world of the local mind. The place where we think we interact with solid objects and have outcomes from causes.

To reach liftoff you need to practice what I call 'outward meditation'. Simple and effective.

Begin by relating to the space around you.

Listen to the sounds.

The sound of your partner snoring.

The birds waking up and singing. A train whistle in the distance.

>> Meditate *outwards*. It tells your sad little brain that you know what you are doing. It sends the signal that your external environment is safe from marauders. That it's OK to let go and drift with the tide of thoughts. Soon, your internal clock will begin to work half time.

Stillness arises. It is worth for us now to go back to recall the practice of breathing. Breathe in normally through the nose. Fill the stomach first, then the lungs. Hold the breath in only as long as it is comfortable and count slowly.

One....two....three... breathe out normally and hold the breath out, emptying the stomach first, counting again. If you can hold the breath out, or in to a different count, that is fine. Just do it effortlessly. The reason for the counting is that it occupies both hemispheres of the brain. The left logical and the right intuitive. Also, as you improve you can tell, because the length of time you can hold the breath grows.

As with any exercise it is intelligent to check with your doctor if you have any health problem.

Now comes the magic bit! While breathing, hold the tip of your tongue up into the roof of your mouth. Why do this? There are two exact reasons. In acupuncture, experts agree that the point in the roof of the mouth is exactly the crossing points for the two major meridians. In such way you are closing the circle of your energy.

The second benefit once again comes under the category of reality. Partially insane people who climb perpendicular rocks for no apparent reason are taught, that by putting their tongue in the roof of the mouth they do not experience fear.

So, go rock climbing! Wow! Now you can begin to see the powerful outcome of practicing this form of meditation *every* day.

If you are trembling at the idea of facing an angry partner or ferocious employer do this: Before the meeting take a few moments doing this breathing practice and Bingo! No fears. Guaranteed. That's worth a million dollars right there. If you can coerce your partners or friends and family to join you in this, then arguments are reduced to amusing pastimes.

You will love me for showing you how to do that. Of course, of course, it doesn't stop there either. You must do this breathing all the time. What does it matter if you do it in *public*? There's a law? Sitting in the car nervously tapping on the wheel waiting for that red light to change. Breathe. Trouble sleeping? Breathe.

If you are a New Zealander, counting sheep to bring on slumber may not be for you! Meanwhile you are consciously increasing your chances of survival! But (there is always a 'but', it seems), here is one of my own ideas. Normally when we breathe out we are told that we are getting rid of toxins. This may be true. But, I will take this moment to reveal that I am some sort of a Taoist (you didn't realise?). Taoists believe that whatever happens we can find a positive result in all our actions and the impacts of other's decisions. That's a long way round to say that when we breathe out, we are actually feeding the plants who will react with joyfulness as they simply *love* carbon dioxide!

To fully enjoy the connection to the Information Field of Creativity we will still have to bath the baby, sweep the floor, plough the field, plant the seeds and harvest the crop.

Being totally in the moment, what ever we are doing, *is* the most effective meditation.

Flight 108: Flight Plan, Cockpit Check and debriefing

NAVIGATING

1. Have your logbook at your side. Your favourite pen at the ready?
2. Check that you are relaxed, comfortable. Mental seat belt clicked.
3. Headphones on the ears to hear the music of the spheres, or the commands from the higher self.
4. This flight is to plan a course which is satisfying, achievable and enhances our spirits. It is the story of not getting anywhere without starting from somewhere.
5. Write down the date and the exact time.
6. Where are you physically right now? Describe your surroundings. Write down how you feel about this room, apartment, tree (it you are lounging outside) or train, plane

or ship.

....

7. What emotions arise?

....

8. How would you like to reach your goal? There are several ways to navigate in the world...the first is called 'dead reckoning', where you follow a map, allow for cross winds and watch out for obstructions – like mountain ranges.
The second way is through radar which is generated by a non-human signal (but *feels* safe).
Then there is GPS, a voice tells you each turn to take, each error you make and precisely where you will arrive.
Lastly, there is throwing them all away and allowing the path to unfold as it will.
Which are you attached to? Are you ready to let go and find the fun of a new direction each day? Ask yourself if you have the courage to do that.
Describe the feelings you have when you look at the blank paper and toss away the resistances, the blockages, the false security. Start writing *now*.

....

9. Pause.
10. Next take out the mental map of your life from birth. Can you

really say that the roads have all been smooth and straight? Weren't the biggest bends the biggest challenges, the best outcomes? Describe the wonder of the phone calls that came out of the blue. The work of your spirit, the connection of your soul with your lessons and triumphs.

. . ■ . ■ . ■ . ■ . ■ . ■ . ■ . ■ . ■ . ■ . ■ . ■ . ■ . ■ . ■ . ■ . ■ . ■ . .

31. Killing Fear

In Rogers and Hammerstein's musical and film, *South Pacific*, the character, Lieutenant Cable, is falling in love with a beautiful girl from a different culture. He sings about the fear his fellow soldiers have of being different:

You've got to be taught, To hate and fear,

You've got to be taught, From year to year,

It's got to be drummed in your dear little ear

You've got to be carefully taught.

You've got to be taught to be afraid,

Of people whose eyes are oddly made,

And people whose skin is a diff'rent shade,

You've got to be carefully taught.

You've got to be taught before it's too late,

Before you are six or seven or eight,

To hate all the people your relatives hate,

You've got to be carefully taught!

The mind loves fear. It wallows in it like a giant immovable hippopotamus.

We cannot overcome it just with our mind. It takes a major physical effort. There are uncounted fears, fear of space, fear of closed places, fear of flying…and on and on.

I grew up in the Canterbury Plains. As the name implies, it was as flat as a billiard table. The only nearby lump was a road bridge over a railway line.

Local people, unused to heights called this tiny bridge Mount Semple!

But for me it was insurmountable! No matter how I tried, I found it difficult to walk over that bridge without getting sweaty hands. Years went by until I came to the time when I was not going to accept it any more.

I went to Nepal (*the world's highest mountains!*) and committed myself to climb a sheer narrow path 1000 metres up to Namche Bazaar, the last village at the foot of Mount Everest. I am here to say I saw Everest *LIVE*! I was helped to that height by closely following the heels of the sherpa carrying our packs!

He led us up to a *gompa*, a remote monastery, at 15,000 feet (5000 metres).

Of course there are no telephones there to tell the nuns we were coming. Well, this fearless mountaineer, arriving well ahead of us, completely collapsed in fear when the nuns exactly described to him what we looked like, long before they could physically see us. This was too much for him. Instead of staying overnight, as he had planned, he quickly headed downhill to sleep in the nearest village. I never found out if he overcame his fear of the mystical, but I certainly was cured of my fear of heights by three weeks of walking the swinging bridges and unprotected paths in the upper Himalayas.

Fear also entirely arises from ignorance. In northern Australia, strong young policemen were sent from city stations into the forest to stop activists who were intent on blocking timber cutters, destroying the remaining rainforest. The policemen became entirely ineffective because they were scared of the unfamiliar noises in the tropical night.

Children often have the same problem. Night-time can be distressful, alleviated only if their bedroom is lit with a low light.

32. The Middle Way

The Buddha spoke of the Middle Way.

Sufi's talk of the unanswerable question.

Here are a few words of guidance from a Hindu book:

> *I am neither the mind, intellect, ego nor memory;*
> *Neither ears nor tongue nor the senses of*
> *   smell and sight;*
> *Nor am I ether, earth, fire, water or air;*
> *I am Pure Awareness-Bliss,*
> *   I am Siva! I am Siva!*

The ultimate paradox; the child's endless questioning; the either/or; the yes and no; the desperate need to be one of those who share a secret.

Those who seek the answer will never know it, but those who do not seek it, will never find it.

When we practice DFR we use the specially designed CD, the *Mind Music*, accompanied with a little poem:

Not expecting, not rejecting
Not wishing nor hoping
Neither grasping for, nor pushing away,
Just resting in a quiet, calm, centred place.

Freedom and truth lies in the middle way, the space left between logic and fantasy. This space cannot be described, if can only be felt. Strength comes not from faith or belief, but from experience.

This means that if we want to discover more meaning in our life, then we must focus on the experiences we have been given. Each one of them is an opportunity to learn. It takes courage. It does not mean that my experiences are more valid than yours. There is no person who can determine that. But what we can do, is share our lessons honestly and see if it 'clicks' for us.

Sometimes it is downright awful to be here in this world. Smiling into the face of the tiger does not prevent you from being eaten alive!

The Buddha said: If you wish to play the sitar (guitar), and you stretch the string too tight it breaks. If too loose, you cannot make music.

The middle way is the only sure way.

33. At the End....Living and Dying

I want to tell you a true story which was published in a French newspaper.

A middle-aged man, whether he was lost in love, incurably depressed or overwhelmed by the political state of the world, we cannot be sure, but whatever was the cause, he spent some considerable time meticulously planning his suicide. At all costs he was determined that his plan would not fail.

So, he climbed to the top railing of an iron bridge and swallowed an entire bottle of pills.

His plan was going well. Balancing precariously on the slippery perch he bent down and tied his feet together.

Next he took out a long rope and fastened it so that when he jumped it would choke him.

So far. Fairly efficient.

But, making absolutely sure, he confirmed that the safety catch on his pistol was open.

Perhaps at this time he became nervous. Because he sort of lost his rhythm. He leapt before firing the gun. The rope around his neck tightened and the jolt ruined his aim. The bullet missed his head and cut right through the rope.

That was disappointing.

But there was still the long fall to the river to look forward to. You could say he went into involuntary free fall. And his feet were still securely tied and the pills were starting to work.

That is, until he hit the icy cold water whereupon he vomited them all.

Last gasp. How could he have possibly imagined that a police launch would be cruising right in his path? The surprised Gendarmes hauled him on board, alive but very cross.

If it isn't your time to go, you stay.

What about the North American Indians who are reputed to be able to tell their friends 'ciao' (maybe they were American-Italian-Indians, who knows), but 'ciao' in any language means 'I'm off'?

These people know when they have completed their time here. They are happy to know precisely which is a good day for them to die; they wander up the mountain and leave. Well, I guess if you were aware enough to read the omens, you could make a couple of phone calls, pay any bills (or maybe not bother), kiss the family goodbye and blissfully drift into the afterlife.

What a wonderful way of living and dying! To know that you cannot go until some cosmic alarm clock clicks over, no matter what you do about it.

Have a nice day!

You are here until you have finished. Once the purpose of your life is completed off you go. No point to be wasting bottles of pills, bullets or Gendarme's time.

Ah hah! I hear you say. I could be happy about all of that if you could be certain that the angels were lined up for a sparkling welcome to the state of eternal bliss.

Well, the first thing is, do not believe all that you've read. The Bible tells us it is more difficult for a wealthy person to get into heaven, than for a man to pass through the eye of a needle, or was it the eye of a camel?

Then we read that the meek shall inherit the earth. What a boring place that would be, to be consigned to for a millennia or so! Populated by unsuccessful people and sycophants! If that's the case, I'm staying here!

In my own case I was given a wake up call...or more accurately you could say it was a ' go to sleep memo'. For many years I was a full vegetarian, hadn't smoked and at fifty-seven I regularly rode my bicycle up to 40 kilometres each day. I was supremely fit. So my heart attack was, to say the least, a little bit of a surprise.

Despite the obvious state of my health, one doctor in Cornell Hospital in New York swanned into the room to exercise his enlarged ego to tell me that according to his estimate (*based on what?*) I had a 95% chance of not surviving. He walked out of the ward in a huff when I told him with those odds, I would take the 5%. I'm still here.

Which brings us to the discussion on the research academics have co-opted for themselves. The Near Death Experience (which, naturally has an acronym, NDE, which is used by those who are in the know...or perhaps more accurately...in the circle of the initiated).

There are untold amount of books and research papers on this phenomena available on the web, in libraries and at seminars. There is no denying that people do have unusual experiences when the doctors cannot find their life signs, and yet they wake up. How inconvenient of them! (One of the biggest acts of anarchy most of us do is to refuse to die on cue).

I have to reveal that when I had the undesired experience of a NDE, all I got was a lot of black until I came round to see a bunch of white coats hovering over the bed.

But, thinking in terms of Deep Field Relaxation, looking for the truths behind the fantasy, the idea of travelling down a long tunnel to meet a welcoming party may be more optimism than reality. One thing we can be certain of, is that no one could possibly know what the experience of leaving will be for each individual. At that special moment what you do not need is a fore-programmed belief. Comforting maybe, but guaranteed to head you off with the wrong briefcase under your arm.

Common sense makes it obvious that all of those wonderful stories are being told by those, without exception, who have been issued with round tickets.

It is as though they got to the train station carrying all their accumulated baggage and discovered that the trains were not running because of industrial strife.

Many of these people start re-examine their life and looking for a new purpose.

I have been convinced by helping people leave, that there is life after death, and because of this I advise you not to try to imagine what the journey will be like for YOU.

I seriously invite you not to read, discuss or
accept this most important part of your cosmic life
with others unless they have an open mind, not bent
on insisting they know. Instead, be ready at any
moment to say good-bye and go. We have to prepare
ourselves for that important moment.

Having, said that, I was privileged (what a
privileged life I have had...just as yours, if you accept
it) to be in the *Potala Palace* with a group of monks,
guided into a room which was full of grotesque, bigger
than life-size statues. To the Tibetans you begin your
journey to the afterlife by being confronted by these
ugly, threatening images. The psychology of it is, that
as you unpick the physical body, you can be
confronted by these personifications of all the errors
and fears you have accumulated in a normal life full of

confusions and misunderstandings. By seeing these as beings, you can fully realise that they are simply vapours which dissolve away when you do not agree to their effect on you.

A DFR practitioner trains himself or herself not to be fearful of their own death and thus can help others who are frightened and confused. Not by talking to, or trying to catch the last breath to convert the troubled one into a religious release. Sadly, far too many religious people are so scared of meeting the Great One that they convey worse terror than the poor victim needs right then.

Here's how it happened for 80-year-old Charlie in Australia. It was very early on in my learning time as a volunteer counsellor for the Cancer Support Group in Sydney.

He had been suffering for some months with throat cancer, unable to speak clearly and bedridden. His wife rang and she told me that something odd was happening with him, could I come to visit? (She had no clear idea how I might help him, but she was desperate for *someone* to be there).

She met me at the door and whispered, 'I have no idea what he is doing'. Mystified, I silently walked into his room, sat down next to the bed and took his right hand.

After a ten minute silence Charlie began speaking perfectly clearly. I looked curiously at his wife sitting on the other side of the bed holding his left hand. Her eyes were as big as saucers. He was speaking calmly.

With his eyes closed, 'Hey there's Frank; he's wearing that sweater you knitted for him. And there is (an old girlfriend from his childhood).' His wife whispered to me, 'But both those people died many years ago'.

He talked on for ten minutes, then with a gentle shudder, he turned towards his wife and his throat congested so he couldn't talk properly.

We sat. He breathed calmly. She wore her worried face, trying to penetrate the situation.

Next minute, he turned towards me even though his eyes remained closed.

'There's Tony (describing him) and my mum,' and several others then he said conspiratorially to me, 'I am learning aren't I? I have been here many many times before, haven't I?' There was a shadow of triumph in his voice.

What did *I* learn? When he looked in my direction and when he was able to talk properly, there was a feeling of letting go. Of total readiness to leave. But, as I observed, when he turned towards his loved wife, he shuddered and came back to the 'real' world.

It was a lesson on the attachment of a loved one to this world.

I gave a prayer of thanks to Charlie. From then on, I understood, that close ones and relatives can actually delay one's departure. In fact, there are skills which allow us to know when it is appropriate to hug and kiss and wish the loved one a happy leaving, another moment when the 'shaman' is able to transmit a bridge between the two (or more) realms of being.

In the Chinese world as a person is leaving, the relatives burn one incense stick and one candle to increase the ease of going through, what is essentially a singularly lonely time. The focus has to be entirely on the work ahead of leaving.

The intended traveller does not suddenly leap out of his skin (except through an accident, or a sudden death or some causes which we will look at in the next chapter), he drifts in and out, trying out the new experience for at least three days, slowly disconnecting from the physical body.

What is more, DFR is equally concerned that the living relatives mourn as little as possible for their departed one. As, since we know of the Field of existence, they can be disturbed by being held back.

You can tell yourself you will all meet again. But that is really just a comforting thought.

Instead of wearing black and crying all mournfully, why not send off the friend with congratulations for completing a good life and wishing them a happy journey?

There are only two things in life we can be sure of. The first, is that you are alive and breathing at this very moment. The second, as I always tell sceptics, is that, no matter how 'clever' I have been in helping people through their troubles, 100% of my patients die.

34. Dying not Dying

Jutta lives near Hamburg, Germany.
Apparently happily married to a man who 'was
gentle, calm and content with their long marriage'.

Then suddenly he began having feelings of
wanting to kill her and soon the thoughts spread to
friends and even strangers.

She phoned me on March 20th 2005, to ask me if
I could help, because he had been heavily drugged for
three months in a mental institution and was not
improving.

'How', she wanted to know, 'could such a nice
man suddenly become violent and uncontrollable?'

Suspecting the cause of his trauma, I asked,
'has anyone amongst your family or friends died
recently?'

There was the longest silence on the other end
of the line.

The machinery of her mind had gone into

overdrive. A new understanding had dawned on Jutta. It reached back into all of her married life. It illuminated so much that had never been explainable. It gave substance to the hell of the last three months.

She sobbed out her story.

It was true. Less than two weeks after her mother had died, her husband began to have these fits. The mother had always opposed the marriage. She had caused him legal problems. She maliciously ruined one of his businesses. Had never once spoken honestly about him and delighted in spreading false ugly rumours about their personal life. She must have been a totally nasty package of goods.

I had no need to explain anything further.

Into the silence all she said was, 'my mother...'

My role then was to gently coach her to help her see what she already knew, but hadn't understood. All the flow of conversation came from her. I simply reflected back to her each comment she made. Helping her overcome the repulsion she kept returning to..... 'My *mother*...'

If we want to be truly healthy and fulfilled in our life, we need to, once again look at the clear division between what is possible and what probable.

This means forsaking the restrictions of Western science which so often sinks into greed and disregard of the world outside of the laboratory. It is time to have the courage and the perception of the wider worlds which have survived in the numerous cultures of the world.

For example, it is possible that some of us, when we die, get stuck, focused on this physical, tangible, apparently 'real' world.

After working with this question for many years I came to the conclusion that in 30 % of strange, unexplainable cases we are dealing with disembodied spirits. Those who haven't migrated to the invisible realms.

To the Japanese it is not unusual to make the statement that up to 80% of people suffer from these intrusions. Not only that, in traditional Chinese belief, 100% of your ancestor's spirits influence your every thought and action.

Of course it is *possible*....millions of people cannot all be wrong.... but to move to a meaningful debate on the probability of such things, we have to suspend our disbelief and open our mind to the evidence.

And it is very convincing. Psychiatrists, psychotherapists and psychologists have long known that there are areas of their specialisations which have a deep emptiness. They have very little success with, for example, some forms of schizophrenia, multiple personality, certain phobias and, even more confronting, the reality of hearing voices in the head as described by many people.

As this subject has been researched and the information shared, it seems that the most common signs of possession could look like chronic low energy level, character shifts or mood swings, continuing impulsive behaviour, abuse of drugs (including alcohol). People might experience sudden onset of anxiety and depression or physical problems with no obvious cause. They would be very upset or reluctant to even discuss that subject.

The idea of existence of ghosts, spirits and disembodied entities has been debunked thoroughly. This is the domain of the horror movie and a source of fear and desperation for those who live with the feeling that something is interfering with their lives.

Of course, there is no way of knowing how many people suffer from this because the risk of being put into a 'safe' place, drugged out of the brain and consigned to a lifetime of terrible hair cuts, hospital food and endless rounds of scrabble, is very high.

And so most people just accommodate the

situation and their friends or colleagues may never suspect anything unusual. Very few ever look for help.

Is the outlook all desperation then? No. Trained people can help. The study and practice of DFR is one especially useful way to get the strength to overcome these confusions. In doing that, as usual, what appears impossible, is as easy as watching muddy water settle once left undisturbed.

I feel, as I sit hear writing, as though I want to take your hand and guide you carefully through the maze of religious, quasi-scientific diversions and the modern misrepresentations of ancient knowledge.

Let us assume, (suspending ingrown disbelief), that I am correct, and that there are those who, for many reasons have not left this world.

The cause can be as varied as a fatal accident, an overdose of drugs, over indulgence in alcohol (particularly being drunk at the time of death), attachment to material things – such as a house, devotion to the accumulation of money and, very frequently, over-attachment to a loved one, or a pet.

These thoughts are not uncommon in many cultures. For the Chinese, as we have seen, there is an ongoing need to keep the ancestors happy as they do not leave this realm and they do affect the careers, income and family plans, if they are not kept content.

In Asian countries you can buy cardboard replicas of television sets, cars, houses, furniture and paper money, which are carried respectfully to the temple and ceremonially burnt to be sent to the spirits of the family.

Other cultures, from Russian to Polynesian, practice many of the same ways of ensuring that the spirits leave. One is to cover all the mirrors and shiny surfaces in the house for three days after the death, in case the spirit sees itself reflected and stays.

These traditions are cross-cultural. No matter where we live similar beliefs have arisen and followed for aeons.

To make sure that the spirits will reach their destination, there is a remedy near at hand. It is called, simply, Love.

No, not the fantasy of unconditional love which is as impossible to maintain as frying an egg in an igloo. That is yet another diversion from facing up to the practicalities of getting through life with as few scars as possible. (Try driving on the L.A. Freeway and soon enough, unconditional love for all people evaporates as they attempt to drive you to an early grave).

What we can find and use is love grounded in common sense; in the beauty of nature and the right of each of us to be wrong and to disagree and still be admired for holding creatively different ideas.

All Jutta needed was to remember some act of love, rare as it might be, which her mother had once done for her. On that magic carpet can ride the spirit into the joyous cycle of existence.

Delightfully, exactly seven days after I had explained the essence of Whakapapa and the need to let her mother go, Jutta's husband was released from hospital. Soon she saw that he was back to his real self.

There were no more episodes of psychosis, no more drugs. In fact six months later a phone call confirmed that since that time, they had had the best six months of their lives.

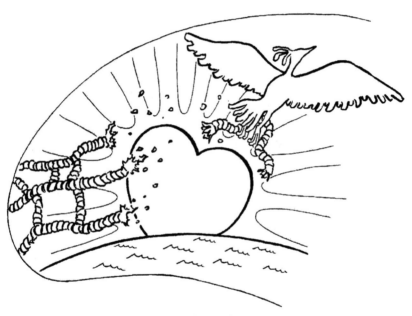

Love, it seems, is all it takes.

In working with the DFR approach - that is focusing on loving-kindness - we find it is not a beneficial idea to investigate the reasons why the spirit stayed. Sometimes it is very obvious, as with Jutta, but other times none at all. It is enough to be there, offering our time and experience as the entity grows into understanding, and the enormous relief of being released from confusion and paranoia.

Our role, then, is to be the arbitrator...the one who provides the handshake between two disparate (*not* desperate, disparate!) parties. Playing the detective investigating the who, what, why and how is a major stumbling block to joyful success.

Explaining how exorcism works in one sentence? It doesn't. Fear has never conquered fear.

Then what about poltergeists? Almost all the literature speaks of the horrors of young girls being taken possessed by entities.

To begin with, there are just as many boys with this problem. And we find that with rare exceptions the 'poltergeist' disappears when some disruption within a family is resolved. Nothing spooky about it at all.

It can be quite simply attributed to the high energy of a pubescent child in a family under stress. In those special situations children have to suppress their subconscious emotional tensions. Which is why it is such a tragedy that so many end up on prescribed drugs - which may be the deep cause of many lifetime illnesses.

I am convinced that the lack of a powerful initiation of children in modern society has taken away the crucial bridge between childhood and their acceptance as a mature adult. I doubt there were many cases of poltergeist activity in 'primitive' societies.

Sometimes both poltergeists and attached spirits combine to distress a family. Jack and Norma were a young couple living in the Melbourne suburb of

Heidelberg. They had two children, Michael (6) and Joyce (4).

Life should have been great! The contrast of what they were going through could not have been more striking.

From the moment they moved into an apparently normal, rented house in a tree lined, quiet street, strange things started happening.

Jack's sleep was continually disrupted. Night after night he would wake sweating, yet the room felt very cold (in summer in Melbourne that would itself be weird!).

Norma began to experience all the 'traditional' effects of possession. As soon as she had got to sleep, she would be woken by the feeling of a pillow suffocating her. Many mornings they would find long scratches on her back.

Their little daughter appeared to be unaffected, but their son's personality changed to be so aggressive and disruptive that he was banned from school.

If that wasn't enough, several times when both children were playing on the carpet in the lounge one of the glass light-shades on the small chandelier would explode. Glass shards would litter the whole room, except where the children were sitting. No splinters ever hit them.

Here was a very rare case of both poltergeist activity and possession at the same time.

I met seven of my students at this house one

evening. After introductions we took a few moments for meditation.

Suddenly one of the students began singing what we learnt later, was an Hungarian nursery rhyme. Norma's reaction was astonishment. She started shaking and crying.

None of us knew that the friend who had started singing was from Hungary and none of us knew that Norma also grew up in Hungary. Incredibly, this was the song her mother had regularly sung to her. Norma hadn't heard it since childhood.

Tears all round.

Next day, *the next day*, Michael's teacher rang Norma and Jack to say that the board of trustees had decided to give him one more chance.

Not only that, the family tensions were forgotten. No more sleepless nights, no more pillows over heads.

The last I heard from them, three months later, all was fine. Nevertheless they had decided to move. The reaction of the Letting Agent, when told they were moving out, was quite unexpected:

'I am not at all surprised that you are leaving. We always have a lot of trouble renting that house - no one has ever stayed there long'.

Poltergeists are almost always attached to people and can move from place to place with them, whereas in hauntings, the spirit remains attached to a place.

A perfect example of a haunting would be a well-known haunted castle. However, it can also happen to a perfectly normal house which people have loved, where there had been wonderful times. Times which were hard to leave.

In these cases, the spirits become attached, sometimes for many years, to the place. They do not wander around but stay in that building, even though they always carry a suspicion of something not quite right.

The fact is, they are like the mouse that roared. As they become more aware of their need for help, the more they rumble the furniture, make things disappear or create illusions good enough to fool the best magician. Sceptics? Pfff!...they *dance* around sceptics, loving the challenge and their amusing pontifications (dictionary, 'to speak or express opinions in a pompous or dogmatic way').

All the spirits need is a good dose of loving-kindness and away they go... usually leaving a nice gift of a new view of the world.

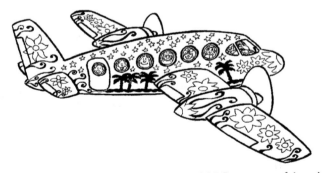

Here is a loving story. In 1985 I was working in the Trigonen Clinic in the lovely city of Stavanger, southern Norway.

Ingrid had grown up in a house which had been in the family for many generations.

Then, later, because of her work, she and her 17 year old daughter needed to permaently move to Sweden.

Although it broke her heart, Ingrid was forced to put the house on the market.

It sat forlornly for more than four years without a sign of a buyer.

She was not exactly sure what I might offer to do, but she had heard stories of others in the city which had seen benefit.

And so, with a sort of desperation in her voice she called me to ask if I could help in any way.

I agreed to meet here at the house.

After some questions and hesitation, she was ready to hear my explanation that it could be the spirit of her mother who was blocking the sale of the home she had loved so much.

Her daughter, however, was not accepting anything of the sort. To her it was all too far-fetched to imagine that her grandmother was still influencing their lives.

It wasn't until we went upstairs to the room which had been her grandmother's bedroom that she started to waver. Because, there, hanging in the closet, were clothes which neither of them had ever seen before. Especially, I recall, a lovely red dress of a type Ingrid's mother might have loved.

They assured me that no one else had ever been in the house. And the heavy locks on the doors and windows seemed to confirm that.

We went back down stairs. Then, as we sat absorbing this mystery, we chatted about the grandmother. I was told that they had such wonderful memories of her love for the open fields and forest around the house.

Sadly all we could see now were houses from the surrounding suburb and hear the sounds of a nearby motorway.

One especially fond memory was watching grandmother chasing away the wild deer who would come and eat the flowers in her small garden. It was obvious that that could never happen again.

No deer could have penetrated the populated landscape we were looking at.

Can you imagine our surprise then, when, as we sat there, a magnificent deer appeared chomping on the flowers right outside the lounge room window.

Each of us reacted at the same time. We all saw the same brown and silver deer. And we were all amazed!

Perhaps we should have sat quietly watching, but the immediate feeling was to go outside and confirm our vision. Of course there was no deer to be seen, up or down the road; neither in any neighbour's yard. Did it send shivers down our spines? Of course it did!

Then we were overcome with a feeling of peacefulness. Whether what we had seen was 'real' or not, no longer mattered.

In the long silence we went inside. Sitting on those comfortable chairs we looked from one to the other. Each of us knowing, without saying a word, that grandmother had visited and now was already travelling on into her own peace and well-earned rest.

Is this just a whimsical story designed to placate troubled Ingrid and her daughter?

Can we be sure that my intention to be of help to them was not created solely in my imagination?

Perhaps. We do not know.

What was as real as a penny in your pocket was that, within the next week the 'unsaleable' house sold.

Flight 109: Flight Plan, Cockpit Check and debriefing

PASSENGERS

1. Have your logbook at your side. Your favourite pen at the ready?
2. Check that you are relaxed, comfortable. Mental seat belt clicked.
3. Headphones on the ears to hear the music of the spheres, or the commands from the higher self.
4. Do your cockpit check. Check the weather. (Check). Do you see any storms ahead? (Check). Plenty of fuel for the length of this long, long trip (Check). Enough stamina to keep on to the end. (Check). Ready and qualified for the journey. (Check). All unneeded baggage stowed. (Check).
5. Check the passenger list. (Who are you bringing with

you?).

6. Put down the date and the expected take off time – expect a delay.
7. Pause.
8. Make four columns down your logbook page.
9. In the left column, put the names of all the people you truly love, those who would be a pleasure for you to share this trip with.

....

10. In the next column - people you know but are neutral to you. People such as your postman, a neighbour, the bus driver. Those who are part of your life but with no emotional connection.

....

11. The third column, the *really* hard one, is a list of people who have distressed you. Those who have hurt you in some way.

....

12. Others – the fourth column. Isn't it interesting, when we speak of 'the others' we automatically think of angels, divas of the forest, aliens, ghosts or spooky apparitions. But if you've been paying attention to the ideas of this book, we have to

agree that there is a lot more than is written in the science or religious - textbooks.

There are wonderful spirits of the ancestors, loved ones and possibly spirit guides who all are sitting up there in the Control Tower, laughing their heads off at our blind-flying antics.

In this fourth column just write one Polynesian word – Whakapapa – it literally means 'layer upon layer'- we translate that into meaning covering all our ancestors, our children, all beings, all molecules, all atoms and all the Field of Creativity.

13. Across the page below all the columns write in large colourful letters:

ISN'T THAT INTERESTING?

35. Survival of the Fittest

And what about Dr.Xu?

I want to tell you about Dr.Xu and the most intriguing coincidence of all.

And the great good fortune of meeting Gloria Loew, an American clinical psychologist and the story of how she became a good friend and colleague.

Yet we already know that there are no coincidences. Just events that arise like jewels of dew strung out on an early morning spider's web. They form with an incandescent glow to hold our attention for a moment, then gently fade to take their place along the intricate structure of the web.

It all began, as good stories should, with a dramatic opening.

The scene is the Intensive Care ward in a New York hospital. Here is a man (me) who is at death's door. He has wires and cables and tubes in all sorts of awkward places.

But what is this? He refuses to be morose. He

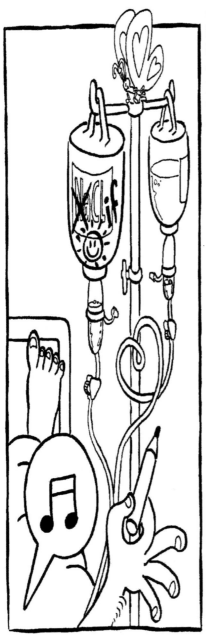

teases the nurses with his ideas of weird healings. He is cheerful, smiling, positive about his chances. He, in short, is not a Co-operative Patient.

More than that, he seems to spend hours just breathing. Odd.

You can see him breathing in to fill his stomach, then holding his breath, then breathing out...pausing...breathing in... 'Good Morning'...breathing out as his body collapses inwards like a punctured football ... 'Looks like nice weather today'...breathing in...

Hmmm...could be a case for the psychiatric ward...he seems to be muttering something... listen...

'breathe in...pump the oxygen into the blood stream. Breathe out enough carbon dioxide to satisfy the plants of an entire African jungle... breathe in...on and on...'

Who could know that I was practicing Qigong, the oldest form of exercise ever recorded? It has a history of enhancing our life forces with the least amount of effort, the easiest way of connecting with the Field of Creativity... that is, accessing the primal source of the All.

But Gloria, already a good friend, usually interested in deep discussions of a philosophical nature was rather more concerned with how to get me safely out of the hospital to recuperate in her spacious home in New Jersey, just across the river from Manhattan. And so Galina and I migrated the few kilometers westward.

Gloria knows about people, what's more, she has always been full of the curiosity of enquiry into new ideas and different cultural mores.

Therefore it was not entirely unexpected that, at an earlier time when I was seeing patients in a hotel suite in Downtown Manhattan, she had arrived full of interest and Life!

She left, after her session, with no doubt in her mind that there was something going on. Next day she came back for another session with an amusing story to tell.

'I am very cross with you,' she smiled, 'because after the session I was so blissed out that I drove four hours in the wrong direction on the freeway and missed being in time for my next patient. I thought, 'If that is the effect of this work I better look further into it further'.

Once again confirming my observation that, if there are no such thing as random events, each of us must be *always* at the right place at the right time.

Comforting thought.

It was while I was working in the same hotel that Jane arrived. (New York, ahh New York, what a wonderful town for great stories).

I did not know at first that she was a news editor for CBS television (she seemed quite normal!). Following my usual practice, I did not ask why she had come, I simply asked her to fill in the small card explaining that I am not a qualified doctor and she should first visit her preferred medical consultant if she had any illness. That didn't faze her out at all and we went into the adjoining room for her time of quietness. She appeared to settle as I placed my hands on her shoulders, but as I moved to hold her head she clearly became agitated. Usually the feeling of someone holding your head without manipulations, without apparent purpose, without intrusion, is the most blissful (see above) thing you can imagine. People often explain it as a moment of intimacy.

In her case, as soon as I finished she was up and out the door like a scared rabbit.

Oh well, win some, lose some, I guess.

Of course, if there wasn't more to it, I wouldn't be bothering to tell you.

Later one of her colleagues, people in the newsroom who daily create stories of tragedy and horror, came to see me too. She told us that Jane had had the incredible courage to talk to them about her experience. Despite her mother's advice not to come and see such people, because 'they' hypnotize their patients, then go through their wallets leaving the victims unable to remember where they lost their money and credit cards, Jane chose to be adventurous.

When she had arrived she had been so discombobulated that she left her purse in the reception room. That explains the agitation I had felt as I worked with her. At that very moment she had been thinking, 'Mom was right. I should have made sure not to leave my purse in the other room, his wife is probably going through it right now! And I am sure he will hypnotize me and steal my pearl earrings, which I should have never worn here...!'

At that very moment, she saw herself drifting up toward the ceiling looking down on her body lying on the bed. That was a genuine spontaneous out-of-body experience (OBE!).

She had never heard about such a thing before. Had it been of any benefit to her? Indeed it had. Among other things, she became open to a spiritual dimension to life. She had learnt the power of trusting her inner sense. What about earrings and wallets? They are not of great importance any longer.

What it reminded me of, was the time when my mind was occupied with the threat of a parking ticket. And the magic happened. Now here was another person whose mind was fully focused on an imagined trauma, and the magic took over. For her, as for me, it was a Deep Field Relaxation *agape* moment (one of wonder and deep realization). And now I am sharing it with you.

When we give the *mind* something to do, whatever else we may be *thinking*, good old nature comes along like a fairy godmother and 'twinkle toes', *bingo*, the pumpkin becomes the jewel-encrusted coach (personal jet plane!).

Of course no one cannot expect the daily attendance of such benevolence!

Even if she is not in attendance you can still have a little magic tool in your carry-on luggage. It is a special *Mind Music* CD. Its repetition of certain rhythm and words balances the mind, giving it something to focus on while not expecting and not rejecting. Just resting in that emptiness.

In reality there is a long journey ahead for those people who are courageous enough to see what happens to the mind.

This is where we turn to Dr. Xu - a small, delicate, intense Chinese cardiac surgeon living in Australia. We'll pronounce his name like the English word, *shoe*. Doctor Shoe. As with many foreign forenames, the true name is difficult for local people to say, and so he took the first name, Jim. Perhaps no one ever felt close enough to explain to him that in English his name sounded like Doctor Gym Shoe!

He had been the senior surgeon at a Chinese

hospital until he was demoted during the Cultural Revolution. He spent the next five years cleaning the toilets before he managed to escape to Australia.

There, he was qualified enough to quickly pass the exams to practice his beloved profession again.

Unfortunately he developed lung cancer and fell in with the western medical methods which left him with half his left lung removed and very little chances of survival.

In this case he saw not much option but to turn to his root culture.

He then studied all the herbs and concoctions of Traditional Chinese Medicine before going back to China to study the art and science of Qigong.

He had grown up with it and remembered it as an effective therapy as well as the best path for integrating philosophy and the physical body.

He knew of the hospital near Beijing which was famous for success in treating almost 7000 cancer and heart patients each month through the use of Qigong.

By re-learning and practicing for up to six

hours every day, he returned home to Australia with a great deal of energy, good breathing and a new lease of life.

Meanwhile, as soon as I was fit enough to travel after the heart attack, Galina and I had also headed for Australia.

What did I need more than anything else at that time? A great teacher and the opportunity to upgrade my study and practice of Qigong, which I had allowed to lapse.

Can it be coincidence then that the very house we picked to lease in Richmond, Melbourne, was owned by Dr. Xu and what's more, he was living next door?

At first it was almost impossible for us, Westerners, to convince this Chinese wise-man that we would be committed enough to the long term studying needed. He knew that many people in the West are convinced that it only takes a couple of weekends to master this craft. If only they could see that 200 million people around the world diligently practice Qigong every day. Anyone who begins to study all the ramifications of Qigong, soon realizes that it takes a lifetime of learning.

Including the study of the philosophy, which is of equal importance to the physical exercises.

Where the martial arts – Tai Ji, Kung Fu and so on – were designed for defense, Qigong is about inner peace through gentle movements and breathing. Truly a delicate dance within the harmonies of the Universal Field.

As our persuasion grew, finally Dr. Xu gave in. At first, four hours of Qigong every day. Then slowly tapering off to one hour per day – but keeping to the special breathing all the time. How delightful, how incredible!

And what a passion! To explain how we happened to meet this man, truly a master, we need to go into the realm of the 'ifs'.

You know them well. The 'if onlys', the 'if possibles', the 'what ifs'?

If only I had not had the totally unexplainable heart problem I would never have experienced what it is like to be completely devoid of energy. If I had not felt that, I could not have truly understood the power of Qigong, nor become a teacher of the *Way*.

What if I had not been fascinated by Eastern philosophies and read so much about them?

How would it have worked out if I had not heard of the Taoist practice of *wu wei* 'action without action'?

If I had not chosen to go to northern Australia to ride my bike (here come the pearls on the lacy web)

I would not have got to Hongkong…or on to Norway…USA…and on and on. Nor would I have found my gift and the ways to share it.

My own development and teaching of Qigong, which I call The Flying Bird exercises, complete the circle of physical, mental and spiritual aspirations. It is based on one of the fundamental Oriental views of the universe.

In poetic language. Correct Breathing, Effortless Movements and Clear Intention are known as *The Three Heavenly Pearls.*

They are the most essential tools for understanding and experiencing the unity with nature, the Universe and *All That Is.*

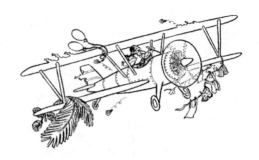

<u>Flight 110: Flight Plan, Cockpit Check and debriefing</u>

REACHING FOR THE STARS

1. Have your logbook at your side. Your favourite pen at the ready?
2. Check that you are relaxed, comfortable. Mental seat belt clicked.
3. Headphones on the ears to hear the music of the spheres, or the commands from the higher self, listen to the *Mind Music.*
4. Do not put the date or the time at the head of this page.
5. From now on we are going to fly without visible support.

We are really going out into space. Gliding weightlessly.

We have gone beyond the chattering noises of the mind. Out where the silence allows us to breath the nectar of not knowing, hearing the movement of the senses, being at ease with seeing the *All In One*.

From now on our log will show that our regular entries arise in the pure currents of the universal laws of unity.

Laws that have been demonstrated through the wisdom words of the Buddha - overcoming suffering by acknowledging suffering; the feminine principle of Quan Yin; through Krishna - the battle field is the mind; Lao Tse - everything works out for the best if you let it; Tolstoy - the Kingdom of God is within you; Jesus - love your neighbors as yourself; quantum physics - if you move, I move.

And Clif? What does he say?

'I don't know'.

'I just know I am doing the best that I can'.

36. Reminders

>> Buy a good strong notebook to keep all your ideas warm as they arise.

>> Once you have scribbled down the ideas into the notebook, it might be fun to get a genuine Pilot's Logbook. In that you can develop your thoughts and spend quiet time just recalling the 'feelings'. These references are so valuable to come back to months or years later...most of us forget those small, interesting details.

>> Get into the habit of making notes at all times. The great thing is to look back in years to come and see just how far you *have* come!

>> Inside the front cover of your notebook paste a photo of yourself (not a group photo please) from a time when you were really happy. Each time you open the book, smile to yourself!

>> Remember about Tulip? It doesn't have to be just every time you go somewhere. This is the fun of it. Off to the movies? Call up Tulip on the direct line and let her know. Driving to the supermarket? Give her a call! Waiting in line, think about Tulip. Sometimes she is off duty. Don't be discouraged, try again later, maybe

she is busy rearranging the Universe a little. So, don't be specific at first. Just watch what happens. Be sure to acknowledge it, if she 'delivers'.

>> The best way to begin 'letting go' is to start with the things nearest to you. No, that doesn't mean partners, friends and family. It means all those little habits that arise which are comforting, but not essential to happiness or easy living. Look at the everyday things. Sit quietly and make a list of things which can be changed easily - don't start with dreams of moving into a castle, or winning the lottery! Move the bed, the cutlery, the times you go to bed or get up or places you go on holiday. Keep a note of when and why you feel upset, angry or just plain out of sorts.

>> Mantras also help to let go of ordinary thoughts which make us overactive and unfocused. Chanting is good for the release of tensions and ingrained beliefs. Do it out loud. The longer you do it, the better it becomes. A good idea is to find two or more friends and chant together.

>> Remember to write this down: *'I am doing the best that I can.'*

>> Try, *'Isn't that interesting'*. See how immediately the effect can be used when you need to defuse an argument, or you are puzzled why everything seems to be going wrong.

>> The first thing to avoid is trying too hard to be 'spiritual'. We are here to learn how to be of service to others. Not only that, your *return to joy* depends on it.

>> Think in terms of *contagious proximity*. Our emotional state will be *transmitted* non-verbally to any person, anywhere. Next time your partner or a working colleague is angry, upset or argumentative, stop and look at how it affects your own mood. If I am calm, you will become calm. Positive emotion overcomes the negative, if you are aware of that.

>> Our individual input is crucially important to the state of the Field! Just as with a telephone connection this is a two-way line.

>> Every morning wake up and count your blessings. Say 'thank you' loudly (all sounds are registered in the Field), wish good health to anybody you can think of.

>> The only moment we know is *Now*.

>> To get out of depression, make *any* decision within moral and ethical beliefs, and then let go of the outcome. Keep content by remembering that you can never know exactly the outcome of any decision you make.

>> '*Going with the flow*' is another way of agreeing to be connected to the Universal energy, to the ever-changing Field. Moving with that wave we can easily achieve the state of *wu wei* – 'action without action', 'non-doing'.

>> We need to admit that no one can know precisely the cause nor the remedy for somebody else's problems.

>> To know 'yes', we first need to know 'no' and a few 'maybes' as well. Keep a page in your logbook to add any 'noes' that you can think of. But no 'buts'.

>> Breathing in the Qi. In a quiet moment breathe slowly in, filling the stomach first to

full capacity. Then fill the lungs. Making sure your shoulders do not lift while your chest expands. Hold that breath whilst counting slowly. 1...2...3...only as long as it is comfortable. Breathe out normally first out from the stomach, then empty the lungs, holding and counting...1...2...3... and so on.

>> Do everything effortlessly.

>> Meditate *outwards*. It tells you that you know what you are doing. It sends the signal that your external environment is safe from marauders. That it's OK to let go and drift with the tide of thoughts. Soon, your internal clock will begin to work half time.

37. Acknowledgements

Bill Bryson has calculated that after just 20 generations each of us owe our existence to no less than 1,048,576 ancestors. Any two of whom might have decided to go to the movies instead of making love at the appropriate moment.

If the Polynesians, Chinese and others are right, then the number of ancestral spirits hovering about are in astronomical numbers.

In short, looking at life in that way, you are one of my relatives. Somewhere in the dark past we have all shared our DNA with each other.

As Jung put it, we are each the result of all the decisions of all our ancestors, and if we do not recognise that we are seriously misguided.

In the broadest sense, therefore, I am the child of a cigar. Unless my great great grandfather had not decided that he favoured a special brand of cigars, and decided to buy them from a particular cigar shop in London, he would not have met the assistant, my great great grandmother, and I may not have been born.

Please raise a glass to the cigar!

Having said all that, I am not so lost in the Field that I would not recognise the living friends, family and others who have participated in creating this book. At least two hundred thousand, three hundred and forty two.

In alphabetical order starting with… Adam and Eve…no I'm joking.

Let's look at chronological order.

Start with mum and dad …good decision folks.

Sister and brothers… like it or not 'someone' arranged a nice bunch of souls to journey with.

The first significant school teacher…Arthur Kibblewhite…who would exclaim loudly… 'Oh, how the mighty have fallen'…if we failed to get a question right.

My first wife, Dinah and my two kids, Craig and Gina who always seemed to understand what I was trying to do more than I did myself.

Friends and lovers. There have not been so many that a separate alphabetical list is necessary. But all have given me parts of myself inaccessible without their – sometimes puzzled - participation.

Doctor Nell Holmes, as mentioned in the text - should I be grateful or annoyed for disturbing my placid unaware world?

Doctor Anatoli Steinberg, whose computer

skills and support have been invaluable.

Roger Dymke, Peter Brinkman, Barry and Caroline McCutcheon, Xaver Remsing, Bernhard Wuthe, Judy and Louis Gebhardt, Maria Padanyi, Agi Bod, Frank Woolf, Jacalyn Bennett, Jean-Claude and Arriane Koven - all students and teachers together.

Special thanks to Baerbel Mohr, a fellow writer, author of the best-selling *"Cosmic Ordering Service."*

Professors Leonid Makarov, Evgeny Stranadko and doctors Gloria Loew, Tony Newbury, and, oh so many.

But I do not want to write just a simple ode to the wife of the author. Both Galina and her son Dimitri took on a world of upheaval and constant change, agreeing to leave their culture, their country and their language for a nomadic Kiwi, who promised nothing except the chance to give themselves to the service of others, and it has been together that we have made all the subsequent work possible. It hasn't finished yet.

38. Reading

Adrienne Carol. *The Purpose of Your Life,* Eagle Brook, N.Y. 1998.

Bach Richard. *Illusions: The Adventures of a Reluctant Messiah*, Dell, 1989. ISBN: 0440204887

Bach Richard. *Jonathan Livingston Seagull.* Avon, 1976. ISBN: 0380012863

Bryson Bill. *A Short History of Nearly Everything*, Broadway, 2004, ISBN: 076790818X

Easwaran Eknath. *Bhagavad Gita.* Nilgiri Press, 1985. ISBN: 0915132354

Fiore Edith. *The Unquiet Dead: A Psychologist Treats Spirit Possession.* Ballantine Books,

Hoff Benjamin. *The Tao of Pooh*, Penguin, 1983, ISBN 0140067477

Hoff Benjamin. *The Te of Piglet*, Penguin, 1993, ISBN: 0140230165

Levi. *The Aquarian Gospel of Jesus the Christ*, Omen Press,1972. ASIN B0006C63RQ

Lao Tse. *Tao TeChing* translated by Stephen Mitchell, Harper Perennial, 1992. ISBN: 0060812451

MacLaine Shirley. *Out On a Limb.* Bantam, 1986. ISBN: 0553273701

McTaggart Lynne. *The Field: The Quest for the Secret Force of the Universe.* Harper

Paperbacks, 2003. ISBN: 0060931175
1995. ISBN: 0345460871

Menses Gavin. *1421: The Year China Discovered America*. Harper Perennial, 2004. ISBN: 006054094X

Ostrander Sheila, Schroeder Lynn. *Psychic Discoveries Behind the Iron Curtain*, Marlowe & Company, 1997. ISBN: 1569247501

Sanderson Clif. *Earth Bound*, Broadview Publishers, 1998, ISBN 0-646-34836-1

Watson Lyall. *Supernature*, Bantam, 1974. ASIN: B000B9EIGM

Watson Lyall. *The Nature of Things*. Destiny Books, 1992. ISBN: 089281408X

Watts Alan. *The Way of Zen*, Vintage, 1999. ISBN: 0375705104

Watts Alan. *The Wisdom of Insecurity*, Vintage, 1968. ISBN: 0394704681

39. Notes on the Author

Clif Sanderson was born in the family of a parson and a nurse/author in the coal-mining village of Granity at the end of the road on the West Coast, New Zealand. Within weeks the family moved to Canterbury, near the city of Christchurch.

This was the beginning of a nomadic life.

During his life he has tried many vocations, from advertising creative director, graphic artist in television and writer of weekly newspaper columns.

Clif even made it to full membership of the Australian Writer's Guild.

He has also published two non-fiction books, *'Making Outrageous Claims'* and *'Dancers in the Fields'* and a metaphysical novel, *'Earth Bound'*.

After discovering his healing abilities he traveled around the world offering his ideas and approach in what later became known as Deep Field Relaxation (DFR) to medical professionals and people interested in this new form of thinking.

The five years working with the sufferers of the Chernobyl tragedy led to further development of Deep Field Relaxation (DFR). This work was recognised by the Russian Ministry of Health with an award for Service to Medical Science.

In Germany, DFR was chosen and accepted as an object of research by the Tumorbiologie Institute of the Freiburg University Hospital.

Please contact him via email at clifsanderson@yahoo.co.uk and visit his extensive web page at www.intention-in-action.com.

40.End Notes

[1] Knox, Ray. (1973), editor in chief, *N.Z.'s Heritage – the Makings of a Nation*, page 147.Paul Hamlyn Ltd

[2] Sheldrake, Rupert, (1988) among his many books, *Presence of the Past: A Field Theory of Life*
* Sheldrake's *morphogenetic field* explains the basic concept of a Universal Field encoding the "basic pattern" of an object. The term morphogenesis came from the Greek *morphe* which means form, and *genesis* which means coming-into-being.

[3] California Agricultural Statistics, Service Bulletins, Fruit and Nuts 1954-1980

[4] Feynman, Richard P, *Meaning of it All*, Penguin Books, (1998), ISBN 0-14-027635-1

* The actual quote was: 'It seems hard to sneak a look at God's cards. But that He plays dice and uses 'telepathic' methods...is something that I cannot believe for a single moment.'

[5] Bach, Richard, *Illusions*.

[6] Makarov, Leonid. Head of the Department of non-invasive electrocardiology, Russian Federal Centre for Children's Arrhythmias. Member of International Association of Electrocardiology, member New York Academy of Science, etc.

The Magic
Mind Music
CD

Sink into silence with the specially produced CD.
www.intention-in-action.com
clifsanderson@yahoo.co.uk
Seminars, Deep Field Relaxation trainings,
Family Patterns gatherings, Qigong exercises

Enjoy the smiles of

Stefan Stutz
Illustrator
www.stefanstutz.de

ISBN 142510560-2